KARMIC L

Examines the esoteric
physical disease and rebirth.

By the same author published by The Aquarian Press
THE OPENING OF THE THIRD EYE
THE POWERS LATENT IN MAN
PRACTICAL TECHNIQUES OF ASTRAL PROJECTION
THE SEVEN RAYS
SUPERCONSCIOUSNESS THROUGH MEDITATION

KARMIC LAWS

The Esoteric Philosophy of
Disease and Rebirth

by

Dr Douglas Baker
B.A., M.R.C., L.R.C.P., F.Z.S.

THE AQUARIAN PRESS
Wellingborough, Northamptonshire

First published 1977
This Edition completely revised and reset 1982.

British Library Cataloguing in Publication Data

Baker, Douglas
Karmic laws: the esoteric philosophy of
disease and rebirth. — 2nd ed.
1. Karma
I. Title
122   BL2015.K3

ISBN 0-85030-299-4

Printed in Great Britain by
The Thetford Press Limited, Thetford, Norfolk,
and bound by Weatherby Woolnough,
Wellingborough, Northamptonshire.

Contents

Part One

KARMA — COSMIC LAWS UNDERLYING DISEASE AND REBIRTH

1

The Karma of Disease

The World of Causes

As philosophers, we say that no effort — right or wrong — that is put into life — evolutionary or involutionary — can vanish from the world of causes. Each life is a result of a unique set of causes and effects. One type of disease may manifest in several individuals, but each individual will manifest the disease from his own unique set of causes and all may differ in this respect.

One of the fallacies of Western medicine is that people are treated according to the outward effects of a disease without giving any thought or attention to the basic disharmony creating the illness, or imbalance.

Each man is responsible for the body he has and he, as a Soul, is the cause of it. Structurally it is, as it were, a condensation of actions arising out of the past. Man reaps today what he has sown in the past. More than this, Man is the maker of his own future through causes initiated in the past.

And by past actions, we do not just mean the immediate past of last week's gluttony — or this week's abstinence — but of causes arising from a past which may go back into many previous lives. Our bodies, both outer and inner, are receptacles for the expression of energies, both creatively and destructively. They are the product of the laws of cause and effect which the occultist calls KARMA.

There is a whole branch of fringe medicine based on this occult law — that psychological and physiological imbalance can be traced in many instances to ancient causes. The case

files of Edgar Cayce, the famous American clairvoyant, bear
testimony to the Law of Karma and show how knowledge of the
real and underlying cause of a disease or condition in terms of
Karma can lead to the dissolution of the most stubborn or
chronic conditions. This explains why some people fall victims
in an epidemic whilst others escape, and why on many occasions
the strongest physical specimens go down in conditions of stress
when their 'weaker' brothers survive.

Cayce says of karma:

In all cases we find, whether they be of beauty or of deformity,
whether they be retributive, persistive or rewarding, a single factor
in common. In all of them the attitudes and actions of the soul in
the past have led to the characteristics manifested by the body to
which the Soul has now been magnetically attracted . . . the body is
far more than a mere vaguely appropriate vehicle of consciousness.
It is a vehicle to be sure — an instrument of locomotion in a very
real sense. But it is not a separate thing, distinct from and
essentially unrelated to its indwelling person in the way that a
taxicab, say is distinct from and unrelated to the passenger that
takes it for hire on a journey through town. It is a vehicle rather,
that is itself the direct product and creation of the worm that spun

it. At the same time, the body is also an infinitely subtle, intimate and accurate mirror. It mirrors both the present and the past — in its movements and ever-changing expressions are reflected contemporary attitudes, ethics and conduct of the ever-present soul and of the Soul's (many lives) in the long-ago past.

Madame Blavatsky had this to say about Karma when writing in *The Secret Doctrine*:

Those who believe in KARMA have to believe in DESTINY which, from birth to death, every man is weaving thread by thread around himself, as a spider does his cobweb; and this destiny is guided either by the heavenly voice of the inner prototype (or Self) . . . or by our more intimate emotional or ASTRAL body . . . which is too often the evil genius of the embodied entity called man. Both these lead on the man, but one of them must prevail; and from the very beginning of the invisible affray the stern and implacable LAW of COMPENSATION steps in and takes its course, faithfully following the fluctuations. When the last strand of our earthly cocoon is woven, and man is seemingly enwrapped in the net-work of his own doing, then he finds himself completely under the empire of this SELF-MADE destiny. It either fixes him like the inert shell against immovable rock, or carries him away like a feather in a whirlwind raised by his own actions . . . and this is KARMA.

(*Secret Doctrine*, Vol. I, p. 639)

He who is the original actor in any trail of events has the most responsibility and karma to bear, good and bad though it may be. Nature will extract retribution to the utmost for what has been done and will reward and compensate in the same sort of manner. All great teachers — H. P. Blavatsky, Alice Bailey, Edgar Cayce, and the Masters themselves — are subject to this law.

Karma is NOT fatalism; it is not Kismet . . . nemesis. Its action depends on us. Each man is his own executioner, each man is his own absolute lawgiver:

Each man is his own absolute lawgiver, the dispenser of glory or gloom to himself; the decreer of his life, his reward, his punishment.

(From *The Idyll of the White Lotus*)

Karmic Laws

In Esoteric Healing, psychotherapy is never complete without the matter of Karma being dealt with generally and specifically by the healer.

It is not possible to understand Karma without knowing something of the totality of man. It would be like attempting an essay on a rose merely by studying its form. This analogy will be enlarged on later and will be seen to be an accurate one as the study unfolds.

Secondly, Karma is better understood if it is accepted that man is linked to and responds to the Universe itself. Karma is one of the laws governing the universe; therefore, this law must also govern man who is a unit of consciousness in that universe.

In the volumes of teachings issued under *The Seven Pillars of Ancient Wisdom*, the writer has gone to great lengths to include something of the totality of man as he dwells within his mental, emotional and etherico-physical bodies. Much emphasis is placed on the importance of man's Soul and the immortality of it:

> The soul of man is immortal, and its future is the future of a thing whose growth and splendour has no limit.
>
> (From *The Idyll of the White Lotus*)

The following quotation from *The Occult Glossary* by G. de Purucker is appropriate here:

> Karma comes from the Sanskrit *Karman* which is a noun-form coming from the root 'kri' meaning 'to do', 'to make'. Literally KARMA means 'doing', 'making', 'action'. But when used in a philosophical sense, it has a technical meaning, and this technical meaning can best be translated into English by the word 'consequence'.

The idea is this:

> When an entity acts, he acts from within; he acts through an expenditure in greater or less degree of energy, as it impacts the surrounding milieu, the Nature around us, brings forth from the latter — perhaps an instantaneous or perhaps a delayed — reaction or rebound. Nature in other words, reacts against the impact of that energy; and the combination of these two — of energy acting upon Nature and Nature reacting against the impact of that energy — is what is called karma, being a combination of the two factors. Karma is, in other words, essentially a chain of causation, stretching back into the infinity of the past and, therefore, necessarily destined to stretch into the infinity of the

future. It is unescapable, because it is universal in Nature, which is infinite and, therefore, everywhere and timeless; and sooner or later the reaction will inevitably be felt by the entity which aroused it.

It is a very old doctrine, known to all religions and philosophies and, since the renascence of scientific study in the Occident, has become one of the fundamental postulates of modern co-ordinated knowledge. If you toss a pebble into a pool, it causes ripples in the water; these ripples spread and finally impact upon the bank surrounding the pool; and, so modern science tells us, the ripples are translated into vibrations, which are carried outward into infinity. But at every step of this natural process there is a corresponding reaction from every one and from all of the myriads of atomic particles affected by the spreading energy.

Karma is in no sense of the word Fatalism on the one hand, nor what is popularly known as 'Chance' on the other. It is essentially a doctrine of Free Will, for naturally the entity which initiates a movement or action — spiritual, mental, psychological, physical or other — is responsible thereafter in the shape of consequences and effects that flow therefrom, and sooner or later recoil upon the actor or prime mover.

Since everything is interlocked and interlinked and inter-blended with everything else, and no thing and no being can live unto itself alone, other entities are of necessity, in smaller or larger degree, affected by the causes of motions initiated by any individual entity; but such effects or consequences on entities, other than the prime mover, are only indirectly a morally compelling power, in the true sense of the word 'moral'.

An example of this is seen in what the theosophist means when he speaks of 'family karma' as contrasted with one's own individual karma or 'national karma', the series of consequences pertaining to the nation of which he is an individual; or again, the racial karma pertaining to the race of which the individual is an integral member. Karma cannot be said either to 'punish' or to 'reward' in the ordinary meaning of these terms. Its action is unerringly just, for being a part of Nature's own operations, all karmic action ultimately can be traced back to the cosmic heart of Harmony which is the same thing as saying pure consciousness-spirit.

The doctrine is extremely comforting to human minds,

inasmuch as man may carve his own destiny and, indeed, must
do so. He can form it or deform it, shape it or misshape it, as
he wills; and by acting with Nature's own great and underlying
energies, he puts himself in unison or harmony therewith and
therefore becomes a co-worker with Nature as the gods are.

The Soul as the Egoic Lotus

The process of the Soul growth is slow and inexorable. It spans
many lives and sometimes even planetary systems. It must needs
be constructed about the framework of the three permanent
atoms of Atma, Buddhi and Manas. Its shape, seen by the
Master, is that of a lotus with nine petals forming three tiers.
Three centrally-placed cusps embower the fiery points of the
permanent atoms which ultimately blaze forth as the Jewel in
the Lotus. The unfoldment of this delicate and glorious
spiritual organism requires time and is governed by law. The
laws that govern the unfoldment of the egoic lotus are the laws
of Karma.

The petals of the egoic lotus are awakened and stimulated
into full bloom by a simple principle. It was enunciated by St.
Paul succinctly: 'Whatsoever a man soweth, that shall he also
reap.' In the birth of a human soul, its seeds are sown and in
the flowering of the Soul, there comes the harvest, or its
reaping. Between those two events there is unending stress, such
as one would expect to find with the budding and blooming of
any angiosperm. It is through stress and through law that the
flower blooms, and it is the same in the construction of a Soul
about its higher Triad.*

The Monad and Spiritual Staying Power

The subject may be approached from another direction with
equal validity. The Monad is engaged through its various
sutratmas with material form. It is through the harsh and
traumatic mechanisms of becoming *disengaged* with material
forms that the Monad gains spiritual staying power. This is
carefully described in *Esoteric Healing, Part Two*, by the
present author.

The Purpose of Disease

Our progressive abstraction from material form is actively

* See *In The Steps Of The Master*, by the present writer.

gained in what we call the disciplines of discipleship, but passively won through eternal ages by the laws of Karma as they govern rebirth.

Disease is a purifying process.* It is through disease that the Soul is able to break patterns of habit that have held it back for many lives. It is sometimes through disease that the Soul is able to maintain its hold on its material form in the face of stress and rapid growth.

In consultations with patients, especially if the case is chronic or even terminal, these points are vital. Sometimes the whole purpose of a disease may be to place the sufferer in circumstances which will enable him to achieve a change of mental or emotional attitude which will permit the Soul a spurt of growth.

As a philosopher, the esoteric healer knows that no effort, right or wrong, can banish disease except through treating firstly from the world of causes. A cause set in motion can only be neutralized by its effect. Even wasted smoke leaves its traces, as sufferers from lung cancer might well tell you. A harsh word uttered in one life returns to you as a rebuke from someone in a later life.

The great 'sin' that leads to disease more than any other is that of selfishness. The Soul can be almost powerless to reach its misguided personality vehicle when it is engrossed in selfishness and then resorts to disease — a process that breaks the bonds of selfishness and purifies its corruption. It is through putting faith in material things that we become selfish, desiring to appropriate objects, people and places, and possess them selfishly. The great Truth expresses the opposite of this and it was for that Truth that the Buddha incarnated, namely: '...that all material possessions must come to an end — nothing is permanent, and he who clings to objects of the world must inevitably suffer when those targets of his attention are removed.'

Even the disciple must make the ultimate sacrifice of his most dear possession, which is his personality ego. The humbling of a personality, its dismantlement and its reassembly about the higher point (spiritually) of consciousness, is the prerequisite for psychosynthesis. Each life we give up a personality in the great transition or change of state which we call death, and death of the physical body is good practice for the death of the personality that comes with psychosynthesis.**

* See *Esoteric Healing, Parts One and Two.*
** See *Psychosynthesis*, by Roberto Assagioli.

Karma frees us from our attachments, just as surely as disease ultimately does. Attachments exist only in astral substance, and astral substance manifests as feelings. A person who is all feeling, all astral, all emotional, is the candidate par excellence for disease, just as he also highlights the fact that he is karma-laden:

> He who feels punctured
> Must once have been a bubble,
> He who feels unarmed
> Must have carried arms,
> He who feels belittled
> Must have been consequential,
> He who feels deprived
> Must have had privilege. . . .*

Carl Jung said:

'The greater a person's faith, the harder he should work, and the work he should do should be for humanity.'

Anyone who joins my ashram is introduced to hard work immediately, especially if he has not met it before. Disciples choked with difficult karma are quickly relieved of much of its effect by hard work in a group cause. Similarly, those who bear their diseases, their pain and suffering with grace and philosophical fortitude reduce the ravages of their disease astronomically. Though this may not necessarily be apparent in the current life, this reasoning provides the best basis for advice given to patients torn by their suffering.

Harmlessness
If a person seems to be caught up in a karmic stream, bewildered and beset with one tragedy after another, the perceptive and compassionate healer can be sure of one thing which will guide him to provide the needed counselling — his patient is most certainly having harmful thoughts, feelings and actions towards other living beings. What can he do?

The practice of *harmlessness* in thought, word and deed must be persevered in at all costs, if the person is to escape the relentless 'reaping of that which he has sown'.

---

* Lao-Tzu, *Tao Teh Ching*, Verse 36. Translated by Witter Bynner.

Thoughts of greed, envy, jealousy and hatred rarely affect the intended victim, returning instead like a boomerang to the sender to wreak their havoc in his life. Such karma, expressing as a disease or a difficult life, can be the result of actions in this life, or a pattern of long standing — surfacing in life after life, until the pain and suffering become so great that the chastened personality finally allows the Soul to live out his intent and get on with the task of spiritual growth.

The Master K.H., in his life as St. Francis of Assisi, quoted these words to guide us in our quest of harmlessness to all:

LORD, make me an instrument of Your peace. Where there is hatred, let me sow love; where there is injury, pardon; where there is doubt, faith; where there is despair, hope; where there is darkness, light; and where there is sadness, joy.

O DIVINE MASTER, grant that I may not so much seek to be consoled as to console; to be understood as to understand; to be loved as to love; for it is in giving that we receive; it is in pardoning that we are pardoned; and it is in dying that we are born to eternal life.

(Attributed to Saint Francis of Assisi)

2

Karma and Discipleship

Causes Set in Motion

In discipleship we practise disciplines that may resolve karma and release us from a backwater of many lives in which the growth of the Soul has become stagnant. Ultimately, when we are karma-less, the necessity for rebirth is avoided. For those who are blind to Karma and Rebirth, disease may be the only way in which the Soul can free its bud. The disciple, on the other hand, by working with other laws of nature, as well as karma, works off his evil and inherited karma by two methods:

1. Self-control.
2. Hard work.

John Richardson, writing through the pen name of William Shakespeare, illustrated the first factor here beautifully in Sonnet 94:

> They that have power to hurt and will do none,
> That do not do the thing they most do show,
> Who, moving others, are themselves as stone,
> Unmov'd, cold, and to temptation slow —
> They rightly do inherit heaven's graces
> And husband nature's riches from expense;
> They are the lords and owners of their faces,
> Others but stewards of their excellence.
> The summer's flower is to the summer sweet,
> Though to itself it only live and die;

But if that flower with base infection meet,
The basest week outbraves his dignity:
For sweetest things turn sourest by their deeds;
Lilies that fester smell far worse than weeds.

Karmic Responsibility

We are all responsible for our karma, as surely as we are for
any debts. But karmic liability increases as we become more
responsible and our responsibilities increase as we become
more spiritual. Cruelty in an animal is karma-less, but cruelty
in averagely developed man must invoke karmic repayment.
When we reach the stage of discipleship, cruelty is almost
unforgivable whether in thought, word or deed and extorts a
heavy karmic debt. Sonnet 94 ends with an emphasis on this
occult truth:

For sweetest things turn sourest by their deeds;
Lilies that fester smell far worse than weeds.

Karma and Discipleship

Young souls, laden with heavy karma, are allowed to take
hundreds of incarnations with only a small share being allotted
to a single lifetime. However, in discipleship, when the decision
is made to intervene in one's own spiritual unfoldment, the
disciple must be prepared to work off karma at a very rapid rate.

Discipleship is a scientific process of doing this as rapidly as
possible, while still remaining creative enough to produce good
karma — to endure suffering and at the same time to be efficient
enough to do good for mankind.

Where a person will cling selfishly to his possessions and even
to his personality ego life after life, lacking the ability to love
others more than himself, there comes the fearful karma of
depression.

Whether we are a president or a pauper, we have to give up
eventually that which we are attached to most. Wolsey's
farewell to greatness from the play *Henry the Eighth*:

Farewell! a long farewell, to all my greatness!
This is the state of man: to-day he puts forth
The tender leaves of hopes; to-morrow blossoms,
And bears his blushing honours thick upon him;
The third day comes a frost, a killing frost,
And, when he thinks, good easy man, full surely

His greatness is a-ripening, nips his root,
And then he falls, as I do. I have ventured,
Like little wanton boys that swim on bladders,
This many Summers in a sea of glory;
But far beyond my depth: my high blown pride
At length broke under me and now has left me,
Weary and old with service, to the mercy
Of a rude stream that must forever hide me.
Vain pomp and glory of this world, I hate ye!
I feel my heart torn open. O, how wretched
Is that poor man that hangs on prince's favours!
There is betwixt that smile (of kings) we would aspire to,
That sweet aspect of princes, and their ruin,
More pangs and fears than wars or women have;
And when he falls, he falls like Lucifer,
Never to hope again. . . .

A whole field of weeds may be outshone by a single flower in its midst and while it blooms and obeys natural laws, that flower holds the position of a monarch to its weed-like subjects. But if it becomes infected, or if the monarch is corrupt, his karmic retribution, by virtue of his increased responsibility, is extremely heavy. Then, the simplest weed 'outbraves his dignity'. The message for disciples is obvious. The simplest worker in his factory is better than a festering president: a Watergate smells to high heaven!

Hard work is intelligence applied, *i.e.*, active intelligence. The target of spiritual unfoldment for the Fifth Root Race is the transfer of energies to the third chakra counting downwards, or the fifth chakra counting upwards, *i.e.*, the Throat Chakra. Hard work is peculiarly a Fifth Race, and more specifically a Fifth Subrace, faculty which relieves karma, not only for the man, but through the man, the karma of the race itself.

Karma levels all. No man, even a Master, is exempt:

Fear no more the heat o' the sun,
   Nor the furious winter's rages;
Thou thy worldly task has done,
   Home art gone and ta'en thy wages:
Golden lads and girls all must,
As chimney-sweepers, come to dust.

Fear no more the frown o' the great;

Thou art past the tyrant's stroke;
Care no more to clothe and eat;
  To thee the reed is as the oak:
The sceptre, learning, physic, must
All follow this and come to dust.

Fear no more the lightning-flash,
  Nor the all-dreaded thunder-stone;
Fear not slander, censure rash;
  Thou has finish'd joy and moan:
All lovers young, all lovers must
Consign to thee and come to dust.

No exorciser harm thee!
Nor no witchcraft charm thee!
Ghost unlaid forbear thee!
Nothing ill come near thee!
Quiet consummation have;
And renowned by thy grave!

Karmic liabilities increase as we become more responsible through spiritual growth. For the disciple especially, mental or emotional cruelty can demand heavy karmic retribution.

Those who try to lead humanity towards an understanding of itself are even more susceptible. If we fail to set the example called for by our leadership, and cause our brothers to regress instead, the karmic retribution will be exceedingly heavy, and the burden will remain until each one has been led back along the way.

The Karma of Teaching and Healing

Even the humblest teacher must shoulder the karma for what he teaches. Perhaps the reason for this is better understood, if we consider that teaching is a form of seduction at the mental or emotional levels, and the actions, thoughts, and even spiritual drives of the pupil may be affected for all time after being exposed to our teaching. We make mistakes as teachers, and people get hurt and the teacher must suffer, then or later. Thus, we are all sons of sacrifice, more or less.

It would seem to be easier to sit and do nothing in some Himalayan retreat, but action for our Root Race is better than inaction, and active service for mankind is inevitable for all neophytes. Any man who involves himself in teaching and in healing others, becomes **bound** to those he has affected and can never free himself until he has undergone all the consequences of those actions arising from his teaching and healing. It is a most serious thing — this trauma of karma — to touch the lives of others.

3

Karma and Pain

Modern philosophies in the West are unable to answer the simplest questions asked by man today, even such basic questions as who we are, why we are on Earth, where we are going from here, and why is it that some people have to suffer so much?

Answers to these questions have been available to the esotericist from ancient days in the teachings of Ancient Wisdom.

Karma and Pain

One of the most perplexing of these questions which have plagued mankind throughout the centuries is why some people have to endure great pain and suffering through various diseases and other misfortunes, and why others are showered with love, good fortune and all the 'good' things of life. Why are some born into this life deformed, or with great propensity to disease or illness in later life and others never know a day of dis-ease throughout their entire life? Why do some have graceful, vibrant bodies full of vital force and others are ugly and full of dissonance?

Science has come a long way in this century, establishing without doubts that there is order in the universe — anywhere and wherever we turn our attention. The planets spin in their orbits according to certain definable laws, revealed by the astronomer Kepler more than three hundred years ago . . . the pressure of the blood in our arteries and veins rises and falls according to laws we can correlate to other bodily systems . . . the whole flowering of the planet earth is woven within the tapestry of seasonal changes by certain well-known laws of nature.

But for all its knowledge of the ordered structure of things throughout our universe, science still refuses to admit that there must then be laws which govern the kind of body with which a person is born and the kind of environment into which that body is thrust at birth.

Of further concern is the failure of science to admit that there must also be laws which govern how we are to leave this life, and laws to say what will happen to our consciousness after we are dead.

Answers in the Ancient Wisdom
The teachings of Ancient Wisdom reveal that just as there are laws that govern the universe, the atom, and nature itself — so there are laws that govern man's existence in that universe as part of nature, and containing atoms as part of his own constellatory beingness . . . the karmic laws governing disease and rebirth.

It is only through acceptance of the fact of karma and reincarnation in our philosophies of today that answers will be given for everything that exists on this planet. These philosophies can then explain fire-walking, hypnotism, materialization, spirit healing — indeed all phenomena of the inner worlds.

The Teachings of Buddha
When the Buddha, a Sixth Rounder, came to the planet Earth, which is in its Fourth Round, it was like taking an Einstein and putting him to work as a galley slave in ancient times.

The Buddha came to teach man that suffering and pain are inevitable . . . that it is part of the karmic role of this planet . . . that a correct attitude towards suffering will help men to deal with it.

A young woman, having lost her first-born, was so beset with grief that she wandered through the streets, pleading for some magic medicine to restore life to her child. Some turned away from her in pity; some mocked her and called her mad; none could find

words to console her. But a wise man noting her despair, said:
'There is only one in all the world who can perform this miracle.
He is the Perfect One, and resides at the top of the mountain. Go
to him, and ask.'

The young woman went up the mountain and stood before the
Perfect One and beseeched, 'O Buddha, give life back to my child.'

And Buddha said, 'Go down into the city, from house to house,
and bring me a mustard seed from a house in which no one has
ever died.'

The young woman's heart was high as she hastened down the
mountain and into the city. At the first house she visited, she said:
'The Buddha bids me fetch a mustard seed from a house which
has never known death.'

'In this house many have died,' they told her. So she went to the
next house, and asked again. 'It is impossible to count the number
who have died here,' they replied. So she went to a third house
and a fourth and a fifth, and so on through the city, and could not
find a single house which death had not at some time visited.

So the young woman returned to the top of the mountain.
'Have you brought the mustard seed?' the Buddha asked. 'No,' she
said, 'Nor do I seek it anymore. My grief had made me blind. I
thought that only I had suffered at the hands of death.'

'Then why have you returned?' the Perfect One inquired. 'To
ask you to teach me the truth.' she said. And this is what the
Buddha told her: 'In all the world of man and all the world of
gods, this alone is the Law: all things are impermanent.'

Human beings have many more than five senses. One of
these is the sense of pain and the physical body has many
sensory organs to register pain — there is even a special tract in
the spine for this purpose.

The Value of Pain

Pain can be remedial once we accept it and get on with our
Soul's purpose for experiencing it in a particular incarnation.
Endured with patience and graciousness of being, then spiritual
growth can be released as a 'torrent from heaven's gates'.

Pain is an experience shared by all living things on our
planet. Cleve Backster has shown in monitored scientific
research that when a plant is approached by someone intent on
burning it with a lighted cigarette, the leaves of that plant start
reacting long before the person reaches it. Once, caught in a
long and tedious laboratory experiment, he grew hungry and
decided to eat a couple of eggs from a group he had just rigged

up to reactors. Not only did all of the eggs show a decided jump on the scale registering pain reactions — but all the plants in the laboratory as well! Plants have some sort of sensory equipment capable of feeling and registering the highest of human emotions: love and compassion. They respond to it and phenomenal growths have occurred when plants are so 'loved' and attended to.

Until man in the West understands the real significance of death our philosophies will remain incomplete.

These lost aspects of philosophy were summed up by Madam Blavatsky in a statement: 'Suffering is heaven's mercy for the spiritually sick.'

We must not think that all suffering is to be avoided. In the West especially, the use of drugs — or whatever can be done to eliminate the experiencing of pain — is the unquestioned treatment of patients who seek medical care. Fortunately, only about 5 per cent of all sick people go to doctors when they are suffering. Most individuals with emotional and mental imbalances make necessary adjustments in daily regimes such as diet, work and rest periods, extra-curricular activities, etc.

In many instances we do have to suffer during traumatic circumstances such as losing a job, having a loved one die, and other life impacts involving severe changes and adjustments. But we do not go running to the doctor for a drug to ease those kinds of pain . . . or we shouldn't!

Who are the Spiritually Sick?

The materialists of the world are the spiritually sick, those individuals who are warped by their excessive attachment to and pursuit of the objective things of the outer world, while at the same time their inner or subjective world is being starved for attention and care. This state of affairs will persist until pain comes into their lives. To the individual materialist, it can begin with a sharp physical pain in a vulnerable site — vulnerable because it, too, has been progressing to that condition in undeviating application of certain laws of cause and effect. To the materialist nation, hundreds of thousands may be struck with pain, suffering and death by a natural holocaust.

Then what happens? Churches are filled to overflowing with the survivors trying to find a meaning behind all this suffering and pain which has been 'let loose' in their lives. Church officials can only murmur that 'it must be the will of God'. Esotericists of the world can point out that it is more the 'will of the people' who are now reaping 'what they have sown' in the great cosmic drama of cause and effect — the karmic law of retribution on a massive scale.

Suffering is Useful

One of the concepts that people will have to accept in a complete philosophy is that suffering can be useful to the Soul. Frequently, the Soul chooses a life wherein great suffering will be undergone in order to heal a portion of itself, i.e. a personality expression that has become too materialistic. If life after life is spent in obstinate refusal by the personality to express the soul's purpose for each incarnation, then drastic action will be taken by the Soul, to force the personality to overcome the blockages to spiritual evolution. What these measures are and the extent to which they are imposed are meted out according to the karma of the individual.

Trial and Error

All of us accept the premise that we learn by 'trial and error'. We even accept that animals can learn under this system of experience. Once we accept reincarnation as a premise, we can then accept that even our lives on earth can be a series of 'trial and error'.

Through the 'trial and error' system carried out over a span of hundreds of lives, we begin to distinguish the true from the false, finally focusing on discriminating the real from the unreal when we begin to tread the Path of Discipleship.

Dispersing Difficult Karma

One way in which difficult karma may be offset is for the individual to merge his consciousness with others in a group effort to provide a service to mankind.

This is especially true for the Aryan race populating earth at this time. As a global entity, our Fifth Sub-race has the specific task to unfold the planetary Throat Chakra under the auspices of the Third Ray of Active Intelligence: groups of servers throughout the world are developing the ability to apply intelligence actively through hard work for the benefit of mankind.

In this way, each individual can help lighten the load of the planetary karma, for all are subject to these laws, even the planetary Logos Himself.

It is said that this high Being is rapidly approaching His own initiation, having satisfied the Law of Karma in His own life to this point of achievement. But just as millions of disciples have contributed by shouldering their share of the pain and suffering of the world, so too will they share in the glory and elevations of consciousness through that momentous occasion.

Part Two

LAWS OF REINCARNATION

4

Death and Rebirth

It is understanding the natural laws which flow from the world of the 'real' that explains to us the nature of the Laws of Karma and of Reincarnation.

Laws of Birth and Rebirth

Your own life is the result of a unique set of causes and effects. The pepper plant does not give birth to roses, nor will sweet jasmine turn into thistle. *Law governs all.* Even the scientist recognizes just this. He emphasizes that law governs the movement of planets in their orbits. Law dictates the times of the eclipses, the rising of the sap in trees, the pressure of blood in human veins. If these are true, why should there not be laws governing how and when we are born, how and when we die, and laws governing the interim period between life and death?

For the occultist, laws like those which govern karma and rebirth are very real. It is only when the disciple truly understands that there is *no such thing as death* but only a change of state that the majestic processes of karma are properly understood. He then begins to perceive rebirth merely as the opening of a door in which the Self passes from one room to another in the dwelling place of the Soul. Actions set in motion in a front room may have to await their resolution until re-entry into that room is made in a life specifically chosen for that purpose.

The Laws of Karma and Reincarnation do not affect our personalities as much as they affect our souls. We feel that we are influenced by previous lives. This is true, but the laws of karma apply not so much to man's lower nature, but to the eternal part of man — his Soul.

The Higher Triad and the Lower Triad
To an esoteric scientist, man's lower nature is a triplicity — a triad made up not only of the physical body which we know so well, but also containing inner vehicles which we also know well on other levels of consciousness.

The Etheric Body of Man
Every human being has an energy counterpart, known in esoteric parlance as the etheric body — which is at long last being investigated by scientific instrumentation. It is this body which yogis say energises the physical body through great streams of energy coming from the sun known as prana — a solar energy that enters through certain force-fields or centres in the etheric matrix, proceeding from there to the physical form.

An Emotional or Astral Nature
Of course, man has an emotional nature — an astral body — made up of emotional substance. Many people hardly respond to anything else, being so controlled by the over-stimulation of these energies as to be considered a 'bundle of nerves' or a 'walking powder keg'.

When we go to sleep, we transfer our consciousness from the physical brain into the astral body, which may then leave the physical body in bed and be transported through the ether in search of targets of people or places . . . usually in response to events or requests registered during the previous day's activities in the objective world.

The Mental Sheath
The mental body of man also interpenetrates with the others. The totality of this interaction makes up what is referred to as the human aura — a magnetic force-field of energy surrounding each person in an oval shape, varying in depth according to the spiritual status of the individual.

We spend so much time developing these bodies life after life only to discard them each time at death.

Karma and reincarnation imply justice and love in everything. No matter how straight the gate . . . no matter how rough the road, we *are* the masters of our fate — if we regard ourselves as Souls. If we think of ourselves only as personalities, then the road will always seem rough . . . the mountain top will always seem just beyond the horizon. Life truly becomes interesting when seen from the plane of the Soul . . . when we begin to control our own karma.

Even a planetary Logos has certain karma to work out, and every living being on this planet shares in that karma to some extent. All of us, from those exalted Beings down to the lowliest of human beings, can begin to control our karma — both good and evil.

Sometimes, the individual fails to learn the lesson for which a particular circumstance was supposed to provide an opportunity. Life after life may be squandered, until the person recognizes the *cause* behind the recurring circumstances in each life. In some instances, it may be many lives before the individual is called upon to make retribution for something he initiated in a life of ancient origin.

Life is a Sine Wave
On one level, each life operates as a sine wave of energy — flowing from birth through death. On a higher turn of the spiral, the wave would show as a continuous journey by the Soul in its effort to achieve perfection, with the peaks representing the travel through time and space in physical forms on the plane of the earth and the valleys standing for the periods spent in devachan.

On a still higher turn of the spiral, an individual can spend a final series of incarnations in several lives with only short periods out of a personality form, with the entire series seen as one sine wave. Such a run would emerge from an extended period of absence from the earth plane (known as a pralaya) and be impelled under the driving force of the Will-to-Be of the Logos to continue in each life the work started in the previous one. Such work would, of course, be on a planetary scale and evolutionary in content — such as a development of the healing arts.*

The Will-to-Be of the Monad would be the driving force for most incarnations. In rare instances, such as suicides or extreme debauchery, the desire of the personality to maintain

---

* See *The Psychology of Discipleship*, pp. 80-83, by the present writer.

its hold on the earth plane can be so strong that the individual is swept back into incarnation almost immediately. Of course, in the latter case, the same set of circumstances would present itself until the personality learned its lesson and escaped from the self-created prison of cyclic events.

But this lower triad of man is transient — a form which we discard at death, which the esotericist knows to be only a stage of consciousness wherein each person enters greater fields of opportunity for Soul experiences.

Certainly this lower triad of man is affected by the Laws of Karma and Reincarnation, but those laws are hardly understandable in terms of one short life. Karma and reincarnation must be evaluated in terms of the higher triad of man — the true, perpetual, enduring part of man — the part we call the Soul. The Soul of man is formless, but made up of three major energies known as Atma, Buddhi and Manas.

When we talk about karma, we are talking about laws which govern ultimately the unfoldment of the Egoic Lotus. This higher part of man which persists after death has been sometimes depicted as a lotus, each petal being unfolded according to the Laws of Karma. Each incarnation is chosen by the Soul according to which petal is to be unfolded in that life — whether it is to be a Sacrifice Petal as the result of great effort in service to mankind, a petal of Knowledge, or a petal of Love. All of this is decided by the Laws of Karma and Reincarnation.*

* See *The Jewel In The Lotus*, pp. 139-149, by the present writer.

5

Dead or Buried Alive?

Here in the West, we know practically nothing about death. Until very recently, we did not even know what constituted the difference between a live body and a dead body. For years and years we have expected that when a person died, it was sufficient to be certified dead by the attending physician. The doctor usually just pulled the eyelids open, noting no reaction to light . . . felt for the heartbeat, which seemingly had stopped forever . . . saw that there were no brain radiations being given off . . . tested for any signs of breathing . . . then: 'off to the mortuary!'.

The Ancient Wisdom has warned for many years that this superficial examination of a body lying inert and to all outward appearance devoid of life systems, is not enough to consign it to a mortuary . . . that in many instances, men may lie in a death coma and may not be able, due to the breaking of the life thread, to register activity in the areas of the lungs, heart, etc., wherein it is anchored. However, the consciousness thread may still be intact in its anchoring in the third ventricle of the brain, and as long as *it* retains its hold on the physical vehicle there is a possiblity that the Soul may reattach its life thread to the heart and resume its expression in that earth form for a while. True death does not occur until *both* these threads have been withdrawn from the body.

In a Coma, but Not Dead!
In many of these instances, the person may not be able to bat

an eyelid or to show life movement of any kind in the physical body — all the while being fully conscious and aware of everything that is being said or done at the time.

> Though his heart gives no beat, though his pupils refuse to dilate to light, though his brain gives out no waves which can be registered, though he breathes not . . . that man may be still alive — and CONSCIOUS!

The author warned about this in 1960 over an American radio show — relating an incident during the Arab-Israeli war, when four young soldiers were found on the battlefield exhibiting a total lack of the four criteria of livingness outlined above. These young men were placed in some surplus heart-lung machines as an experiment and their blood was kept in normal circulation. After a period of two weeks, the hearts of all four young men began to beat on their own, the brains became alert, and they recovered sufficiently to be removed from the machines and take up regular convalescence.

In 1962, a funeral procession won wide coverage in the French press. As the coffin was being carried to the grave site, scraping noises were heard inside, whereupon the coffin was opened. The body was discovered to be still warm but by this time fully deceased. There was such an uproar following this disclosure, that the medical profession was asked to make a statement. The spokesman for that august body of men stated that at least one person in 500 was buried alive in France, under somewhat similar circumstances.

In several thousands of years, man has hardly progressed in his concepts of death. Primitive man may have described an eclipse of the sun in terms of some great beast having swallowed up the flaming orb from the skies, and when the eclipse was over, he might have said that that great beast had finally disgorged the sun back into the heavens.

This may seem silly to us today, but modern man is not much better in his knowledge about the eclipse of man from earthly life on this planet — in what we call death.

Man undergoes an eclipse from form life during death. There is a temporary obscuration of what we call the physical body, and once more — in a later incarnation — man reappears, unaffected by that previous death except as the final experience in the entire life cycle.

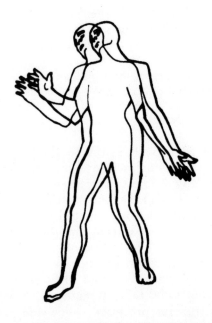

Doctors in the United States, Canada and the United Kingdom especially are becoming concerned with the criteria which determines the true death of a person because they do not wish to take organs from a living person to transplant into another. But how can it be possible to be absolutely certain that the person is beyond recall to physical life?

During 'death' states, many people have reported having out-of-body experiences, and these utterances from normal and sane people give us pause to think:

There is another group of people having out-of-body experiences which is worth mentioning. It is those rare individuals who suffer clinical death. During a heart attack or whilst undergoing surgery, someone occasionally 'dies'. By this we mean that the heart stops and to all intents and purposes, the person is dead. If or when he is successfully resuscitated, he frequently reports an out-of-body experience which is astral projection pure and simple whilst the physical body lies 'dead' on the operating table.

Leslie Sharpe, a Toronto businessman had just this experience. Late one spring afternoon in 1970, his heart stopped beating and for three minutes and eleven seconds, he was 'dead'. But he survived and recalled, in vivid detail, his sensations during clinical death. I quote now from the report by the *Toronto Daily Star* columnist Sidney Katz. . . .

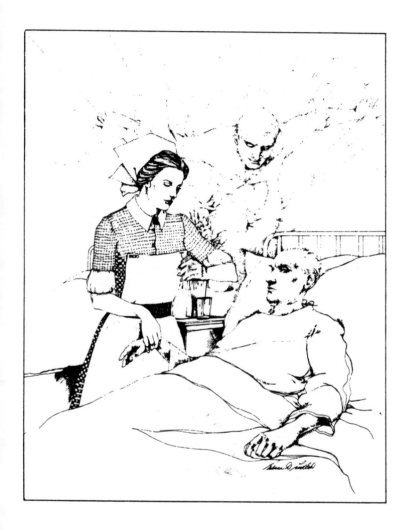

'I saw myself leave my body, coming out through my head and shoulders. The body was somewhat transparent, although not exactly in vapour form. Watching, I thought, "So this is what happens when you die."'

Upon recovering consciousness, the first thing he told the doctor at his bedside was: 'If I go out again, don't bring me back — it's so beautiful out there'.

'I saw myself leave my body, coming out through my head and shoulders. The body was somewhat transparent, although not exactly in vapour form. Watching, I thought, "So this is what happens when you die."'

The scene suddenly shifted and Sharpe now found himself sitting on a small object, tilted at a 45° angle, travelling through a blue-grey sky at a great speed . . .

The next sensation was of a 'delightful floating' in a bright yellow light. Sharpe recalled: 'I have a scar on my right leg, the result of an old injury. Although, at the time, I was not conscious of having any lower limbs, I felt the scar being torn away and I thought, "They have always said that your body is made whole out here. I wonder if my scars are gone?".'

Man on this earth has conquered many fields. He has climbed the highest mountains on this planet . . . plunged to the oceans' depths . . . journeyed into the regions of the skies . . . even walked on the moon. All of these fields of endeavour have been investigated by man with great success, but there is one vast area of man's experience which he knows little or nothing about. This is the hidden factors behind disease and death.

Instead of having a wholesome, joyous and happy attitude to this transition in consciousness which we call death, there is expressed everywhere on this planet a great fear and horror of this most natural of events.

Still to this day, black is worn and it was not so long ago that there were plumed horses dragging the funeral bier to the grave, with all the paraphernalia which each civilization has deemed it proper to display in the drama of departure from the physical plane. At least this is so in the Western world. The oriental has a different view on life after death, and it is because of this that such places as Bangaladesh and China and India can withstand such terrible cataclysms . . . can bear them and resolve them, emerging undaunted from the holocausts to rebuild anew with great courage and perseverance in the face of overwhelming odds.

People in North America still talk about the great San Francisco earthquake at the beginning of the century as if it were nearly the end of the world. There have been thousands of geophysical episodes of this magnitude in the Far Eastern countries even in the last few centuries alone, and their ability to survive has stemmed in large part from the attitude the people have towards death.

The Church and the Doctrine of Reincarnation

Reincarnation was once accepted by the Christian Church and was part of the early churches' teachings. About three or four hundred years after the life of Christ, the church rejected 'reincarnation'. Perhaps it was because people became lax in their spiritual growth, thinking they could enjoy the 'good things in life' and put off all the effort 'required' for spiritual evolution. For whatever reason, it was stricken from the Church doctrines and ignored down through the centuries.

For most people concerned with their spiritual evolution, a recognition of the Laws of Karma and Reincarnation merely spurs them on to greater and greater efforts. When work is meritorious, when it is service to mankind, when it is evolutionary, then the disciple or initiate knows that he can come back in another life and get right back on the same job.

Life in Terms of Justice and Love

The Laws of Karma and Reincarnation help us to see all life on this planet in terms of justice and love. If a child of three or four dies in her mother's arms, screaming with the pain of cancer of the bowel, God is not to be blamed: this can be a karmic justice working out for that Soul in a strange way. That Soul chose just that life in order to come back in a later incarnation without the necessity of undergoing such heavy karmic retribution — with freedom to experience a more spiritually evolved life, perhaps to serve humanity in a unique and exalted manner.

Part Three

SOME DISORDERS AND THEIR KARMIC CAUSES

6

Psoriasis: A Change of Soul Ray Needed

'I was consumed with embarrassment', 'I nearly died on the spot'. These are common phrases used to express the uncomfortable feelings of not infrequent individuals who live lives of great emotional sensitivity, who seem to eternally be discomforted by every situation that develops. This is carried from life to life until it becomes a serious impediment in the Soul's aim of 'personality integration' as a preliminary to the Path of Initiation. This condition of life-long embarrassment often characterizes a soul's emergence from a period of recession, of working inwardly at consolidating the subtler vehicles before undertaking a series of incarnations. It may also signal that a change of Soul Ray has recently been accomplished. Thus a First Ray soul, leading inwardly an extrovert life with perhaps a series of thirty-odd incarnations having predominantly introverted personalities, now changes its qualities. The inner life becomes introverted and the outer personalities must become extroverted.

Ray Factors
An example of this shift of polarity from an introverted personality can be given in terms of Ray equipment.* The patient, in the previous life could have had a First Ray soul with a Second Ray personality, a Fourth Ray mind and a Second Ray astral body. In this case the physical body would probably have been on the Seventh Ray:

A.

I	2	$\left\{\begin{array}{l}4 \\ 2 \\ 7\end{array}\right.$	Mental Body Astral Body Physical Body
Soul	Personality		

A change of Soul Ray to Ray Two would necessitate a more introvert personality on a Will Ray in order to balance the Love Ray of the soul:

B.

II	3	$\left\{\begin{array}{l}1 \\ 1 \\ 7\end{array}\right.$

This transition would be difficult and a few intervening lives with a combination of Rays less harsh and intermediate to these would be helpful and transition could be effected with more facility. The Sixth Ray, though also a Love Ray, is far more extrovert than the Second Ray:

C.

II	6	$\left\{\begin{array}{l}4 \text{ or } 5 \\ 6 \\ 3\end{array}\right.$

The Third Ray physical body would be a stronger and less sensitive vehicle, capable of supporting the transition.

Such a process of transition from introvert personalities (and extrovert soul) would be assisted by a life or two in which psoriasis ensures progress. Thus, movement from A to B is via C:

$$A \longrightarrow C \longrightarrow B$$

The change is not effected without some difficulties. Where there is unwillingness of the personality to conform to the Soul's purpose in this respect, i.e. to become outgoing as a personality, psoriasis may manifest out of such conflict. Usually the life is not completely unbearable. Supporting personalities (as a mother or husband) will be present. The lesions of psoriasis, often present in places which are conspicuous, e.g. the scalp, do attract attention. If the patient can with his psoriasis face up to the harsh scrutiny of society for but a single lifetime, this is usually sufficient to round out the serious defect obstructing personality integration.

* See *Esoteric Psychology, Vol. V.*

This karmic explanation is hardly likely to be accepted by the patient as a substitute for treatment or cure, but it may be supportive during those dread periods of exacerbation. The condition should be treated, for even in treatment there is focus of the healer's attention on the lesions and the personality of the patient which is therapeutic both at karmic as well as personality levels. But it is important to remember that the overcoming of excessive emotional response to life situations is the most important hurdle and not the signs and symptoms of the disease itself. If the patient can achieve calm and poise in a life of psoriasis he will never be ruffled by the 'slings and arrows' of the lives that lie ahead and the 'outrageous fortune' that awaits him, for instance, in Scorpio, such as those trials imposed on such hero-initiate mythological and historic figures like Hercules and Rustum.

The karmic factor underlying psoriasis is, therefore, a series of lives which developed extreme emotional sensitivity, a sensitivity deriving its energies from the higher astral subplanes. This refinement of feeling led to an inordinate sensitivity to everything in the environment — people, places, conditions — which frequently shows as embarrassment in the presence of those who are lacking in emotional sophistication. The disease derives from neo-Atlantean periods when such high emotional sensitivity became possible. It is related to the Solar Plexus chakra and to that major group of diseases deriving from Atlantis which come under the heading of cancer. These are never contagious but they are most frequently genetic and inherited.

Care is needed in determining the karmic situation in psoriasis. Only when highly sensitive emotional beings were being evolved was it possible for the disease to thrive. Atlantean stock with the potential for psoriasis began to be used as vehicles for incarnation and the reasons for certain souls with many Atlantean qualities choosing such bodies is given above in terms of Ray energies.

Treatment
There is no cure for psoriasis, which is inherited through a genetic pattern we understand very poorly. Therapy has been known, however, to keep the skin clear of psoriasis for up to ten months. Each year eight million Americans spend a billion dollars on messy and often dangerous therapies. In some,

hospitalization clears the condition only for it to emerge once more on discharge.

New and promising methods of treatment are emerging within orthodox medicine and they hold out hope to the esoteric sufferers because they employ a more natural type of therapy. Recently attention has been focussed on the use of ultraviolet light in conjunction with a powdered weed taken from the banks of the Nile. In ancient days, the material was swallowed by Egyptians who then exposed thier bodies to sunlight. It is interesting to remember that ancient Egypt was a colony of Atlantis.

Magnetism

The use of magnetism has been effective as treatment where low intensity fields pulsating at about 256 cycles per second produce remission but — let this be emphasized — no cure. The use of cortisone ointments is now in disfavour because of side-effects . . . and to this the science of esoteric healing would add its own 'Amen!'*

In the end, the lesson which the Soul of the psoriasis patient teaches must be learned or a later life will have to be used up once more in forcing the karmic lesson on the individual. The lesson is very straightforward in terms of Rays . . . the transfer of energies from the solar plexus to the heart accompanied by extroversion of the personality. The Ray of the personality should change to a Will Ray, i.e. 1, 3, 5 or 7. The manual of spiritual disciplines, *Discipleship In The New Age*, gives techniques for achieving such Ray re-alignments.

In ordinary language, this means the development of a personality that faces up to all the demands of 'living in the world', as well as maintaining the emotional sensitivity won during Atlantean incarnations. Preciseness in everything embarked upon, accuracy in detail, completion of tasks, mental polarisation of consciousness and right human relationships are the keynotes for those 75 million persons afflicted with psoriasis on this planet. All other therapy should be applied with these factors as the governing consideration.

A variety of treatments within the bounds of 'natural therapy' can alleviate the worst symptoms of psoriasis including homoeopathy, biochemics and diet. Far more

* See Appendix I.

important, however, is the encouragement that can be given to
the patient through the karmic explanation for the condition
as outlined above. This will help to lift the patient's attitude to
the level of the mental plane and prevent over-energization of
the Solar Plexus Chakra which lies at the root of the psoriatic
exacerbations.

Chakras

During the periods of exacerbation, treatment should be
directed towards drawing off energy from the Solar Plexus
Chakra. This can be done by suggestion to the patient methods
of transmutation of energy of that region to the Heart Chakra,
the normal disciplines of Yoga being involved there:

Not selfish love, but selfless love . . .
Harmlessness in thought, word and deed . . .
Not attachment but *detachment* towards pain, the
attitude of others, the demands of the marriage
partner, the psoriasis lesions, etc.

During remissions, treatment should be maintained because
the disease is still there. Now, there should be direction of
healing energy from Head Chakra to Head Chakra. The
strengthening of the patient's will, his initiative, his capacity
not only to start but to finish projects, his confidence, etc., can
be enhanced by this energy transfer. The evoking of the Will,
instead of the emotions, will make each attack thereafter less
important in the eyes of the patient. The karmic problem will
be slowly but surely resolved and the patient will be fulfilling
the soul's purpose.

7

Anorexia Nervosa: Disembowelment and Idée Fixe

This is a comparatively rare condition but one which bears lessons for the esoteric healer, for the disciple and for the would-be martyr.

Many of us have witnessed the emaciation of someone with a terminal illness like cancer or with an equally debilitating condition like tuberculosis or have seen the newsreels of victims in concentration camps. It is a harrowing sight and one wonders about the karma behind such an experience, but in *anorexia nervosa* we are confronted with an individual without any evidence of disease refusing food and having no political, social or other comprehensible motive for doing so. The patient will refuse food or, accepting it, will hide it and make every effort to avoid eating. This leads to progressive starvation, malnutrition and death.

Group Karma

One wonders whether the so-called heroic fasting of individuals for political reasons or in social protest are entirely altruistic and whether devotion to the political ideal behind the fast has not become a cause of hysteria and that the rejection of food is part of the hysteria. I stress the example of deliberate starvation for political reasons because, basically, the karma involved here is group karma to the extent of it being national karma.

Some dreadful events have, especially in the last 150 years, been associated with nationalistic, separative tendencies — or to put it more esoterically, group karma on a racial scale. Some souls choose to shoulder this burden and accept incarnations in which there are conditions imposed by the environment of sustained fear, not necessarily through the presence of violence like the threat of air raids, but possibly through a domestic situation where perhaps the father of the family is an alcoholic or the mother has narrow, entrenched views or puritanical attitudes or lives on an insecure income.

The Factor of Sexual Expression

Emotional loneliness plays a part here. Most people turn towards food in such states, but this patient turns away from it. It is an occult fact that powerful sex drives have to be sustained with large appetites for food or, conversely, a large appetite for food can demand expression in powerful sex drives. If the presence of fear is powerful enough, unremittent and a fear that begins early in life, sexual expression (or, for that matter, all expressions) becomes inhibited. There is nothing to 'spend' the energy of food on. Self-denial becomes a way of life. The isolation becomes confused with independence, and eating less implies less dependence.

Where there is an emphasis on nausea in the anorexia nervosa patient, the karma which is involved is most likely to be disembowelment in a previous life.

The Idée Fixe

There is always an *idée fixe*, and according to the psychological outlook, the anorexia patient will become cachexic in distinctive ways. Characteristically, different classes of patients will achieve their cachexia in different ways, although the overlap may be considerable and exceptions are not rare. Typically, the adolescent anorexic will worry about obesity and will diet excessively to escape the ridicule of family and friends. The hysteric will develop somatic disturbances which interfere with the ingestion of food. The phobic will fear obesity and refuse to eat. The obsessional will ruminate about food and obesity, pursue a diet ritualistically and may indecisively fluctuate between bulimia (insatiable hunger) and abstinence. The depressed patient will lose his appetite and develop a disinterest in food, whereas the schizophrenic will develop delusions about food and most typically decide it is contaminated and poisoned.*

* *The Textbook of Medical Treatment*, Dunlop, Davidson, Alstead; London.

Treatment
The treatment aims at reducing the stranglehold which the
fixed idea has upon the patient by constantly emphasizing the
need to release oneself from it. The *idée fixe* should be
debunked and reasons given for it. More important than
anything should be the repetition and emphasis of the advice.

Anorexia nervosa and its treatment always calls to mind an
old but effective method used in Africa by the native inhabitants
for catching monkeys. A small hole just large enough to take a
monkey's paw is made in a melon or kalabash and left as bait.
The monkey sticks his paw into the fruit to grasp the sweet pips
at its centre. The native charge the monkey, who in his panic
cannot release his hold on the pips, and the fist, being much
enlarged, will not pass out through the aperture and the
monkey cannot move away with the melon attached to him
and is easily caught.

The relationship of the monkey's plight and the anorexia's
attachment to his *idée fixe* is obvious.

Spiritual Martyrdom
Anorexia nervosa makes an interesting example of emotional
or astral energies directed entirely into one specific project to
the exclusion of all else, to the formation of an attachment so
strong and so negative to the point of hysteria so that life and
limb are threatened.

One can understand that the same forces at play here could
send Christians into the arena and to martyrdom.

Compare also the condition with that one in which the
WILL — the divine persistent will of Atma — is invoked and
applied, where a powerfully motivated spiritual person fasts as
a heroic example to others, a highly integrated personality,
unruffled by emotions, coolly and with full awareness of
consequences. This calls to mind Mahatma Ghandi.

When Atma is Absent
It also makes us recall the 'superman' effort of the rare athlete
who, under severe stress, drives the physical body along the last
few desperate yards to the winning post against all the contra-
urges of his physical body, mind and emotions, when blood
lactic acid is rising, when lack of oxygen, the accumulation of
carbon dioxide and muscle cramps scream out for relief. This
is when Atma is called down from the higher triad. It is seen

descending sometimes in the last despairing gesture of a Soul to retain its physical vehicle in what we call the 'will-to-live'! No esoteric healer should be unaware of its presence in a patient and evidence of it should make the healer redouble his efforts. Equally so, the complete absence of it should be noted with concern, for it most fequently indicates the Soul's desire to withdraw from its vehicle, the physical body.

8

Breast Cancer: Atlantean Karma

The death rate for cancer of the breast has not changed in thirty-five years. Its incidence of 7 per cent makes it the most common form of female cancer and the greatest cancer killer of women in America today.

The possible reduction of these statistics lies only in the improvement of current methods of detection of the lump, earlier and better ways of applying surgery, X-ray therapy and hormones. These methods have been current stock-in-trade for many years past and the only prospect in the future. No wonder there is gloom. Suggestions that a vaccine can be produced to fight breast cancer are doomed because cancer is *not* caused by virus.

In fact, more American women are developing breast cancer so that its incidence has risen more than 30 per cent in the last thirty years. Two famous victims have been the wives of the two American presidents in office in the seventies.

Mastectomy Gains Little Time

Though surgery has seemed the obvious way out, especially when there is early detection, hopes of survival with surgery have not been so much greater than without it . . . in terms of time, about seven weeks . . . not much to show for such a ghastly mutilation as radical mastectomy.

Surely, with this sort of history, other methods of dealing with the condition, at least over a long term, would be to spend more time and some more of that incredible sum of money yearly given to cancer research, in seeking out *causes*. All causes may not be easy to eradicate — in fact, they will not be for many centuries — but to know them is to commence research on a true and sound basis.

The author writes not entirely with dispassion about this condition. He watched, from the age of eleven, his own mother go through all the traumatic and classical stages of surgery, to no avail, so that he was orphaned at fourteen: the lump in the arm... the radium needles... the lump in the breast... radical mastectomy... the metastasis to the abdomen... the long, lingering processes of cachexia... and death, the final act — a happy release. He feels certain now after many years of introspection that the organ lopping, and all the other paraphernalia of treatment made not the slightest difference to the prognosis.

Causes of Breast Cancer

These exist at various levels. The most widespread and deep-seated cause is karmic in the sense that all cancers form part of the group disease which resulted from the excesses of the Atlantean Root Race as it struggled with the progressive opening and controlling of the Solar Plexus Chakra, that centre which receives the emotional impacts of both the astral world (within) and the world of activity without.

Many of us have incarnated in bodies of Atlantean stock, especially, under the Laws of Karma, those races which formed part of the colonial remnants of Atlantis that survived the destruction of the mother continent, *viz.*, North America and Western Europe. We carry within us (the author included) taints of that stock, which predisposes us to that major group of diseases, one of three, into which category falls that of cancer. Whether the cancer will express itself physically in this life or will remain latent until the next or subsequent lives, depends on the karma of the individual and the presenting stimuli of this life. Those stimuli may be minor ones — such as a high saturated fat diet, underarm deodorant spray, excessive sunlight, high blood oestrogen levels, etc. — or the major one which is *emotional indiscipline*.

In breast cancer there is inability of the Heart Chakra to accept the excessive output of energies from the Solar Plexus as that centre acts as a channel for emotional drives.

At the outset it must be said that at the moment this is a

planetary problem with planetary karma seizing an opportunity to express itself through Sagittarius and its esoteric ruler, the Earth.

In simpler terms, this manifests through emotional blocks, inhibitions, irritations which stimulate cancer in the region of the breasts.

The soul   would count the cost as being well worth it if one incarnation could be sacrificed to obtain emotional integration and discipline, but would regard it even more recommendable if that integration could be obtained by such processes as would not involve the loss of the physical vehicle. All that can be done, here, is to list some of the emotional factors where the lack of control leads to the inherent cancer condition expressing itself through the breast.

Inability to Transfer Energies

Of course, there are also predisposing factors at the level of the etheric body which will decide *what* part of the body the cancer will express itself through. This might be through the cervix of the uterus if there was inability to transfer energy from the Sacral Chakra to the Throat Chakra, or as cancer of the throat or thyroid, if energy could not be received in the Throat Chakra.

The Sexual Factor

There may be an innate shyness and embarrassment with the sexual act, despite years of married life, or a deep and unexpressed distate for the marriage partner so that the sexual demands and conjugal rights are, at least subconsciously, regarded with deep loathing. This inner emotional inhibition may be emphasized through regarding the sexual activities of other women in the same way. Every case of rape read about in the newspaper may, through deep sympathetic rapport or revulsion, center energies in the breast so that overstimulation of physical and etheric tissue results. How often will you not see a woman clutch at her breasts when she hears of or sees something emotionally stimulating . . . perhaps her favourite actor or some horrible tragedy.

'Beating the breast' in despair is a practice not long lost from our folkways. Any acts like sexual perversions or miscegenation on the part of others can lead to deep apprehensions and fear, felt mainly around the heart region. 'Putting oneself in her position' would sum it up.

Any sort of emotional insecurity produces the same sort of effect, especially when it is associated with the husband or breadwinner. The emotional insecurity frequently arises through marrying what might be regarded as someone socially inferior, producing a deep unconscious horror of being polluted. Women tend to react emotionally in the breast region. From an early age, especially from adolescence on, tests show that women aspire to large breasts. All this may seem very mundane and a matter-of-fact part of life, but to highly sensitive women, incarnated in bodies of Atlantean stock, it can be death-dealing.

Re-enacting the part played by others is basic to Atlantean types. This is c..e of the reasons why so many actors develop cancer. They are generally Atlantean stock and theatre gives them the opportunity to *feel strongly* and, incidentally, through accession of such energies to work off karmic debts.

Treatment

What therapy can be recommended? Usually it is too late to start talking about emotional discipline to someone with breast cancer. Certainly the years ahead will reveal that the emotionally disciplined tend to be free of cancer of the breast. All forms of appreciation and participation in the highest and most classical arts give opportunity to learn emotional discipline, especially theatre, music, sculpture and painting.

9

Rheumatoid Arthritis: Stagnation in the Soul

At the outset we should distinguish between rheumatoid and osteo-arthritis. Rheumatoid arthritis is an inflammatory condition which leads to ankylosis (stiffening) of the joints with variable degrees of immobility and pain. Osteo-arthritis, on the other hand, is a *degenerative* disease in which there is erosion of joint surfaces, again with degrees of pain and immobility.

From the esoteric standpoint, they have an entirely different aetiology. Rheumatoid arthritis goes back to Lemuria and forms part of that group of diseases related to the Sacral Chakra, as that centre became the focus of attention for the Third Root Race. Osteo-arthritis is linked to the Atlantean Root Race and forms part of that group of diseases which are of astral origin, in that the inflow of emotional energies from the astral via the Solar Plexus Chakra produces friction which reflects as the disease condition. Emotional imbalance in this or previous lives has led to self-consolation in the form of gluttony or in poor metabolism through ignorance of the finer points of nutrition.

Causes of Rheumatoid Arthritis
The cause of rheumatoid arthritis is not known to medical science. Many theories have been advanced about its aetiology, but these have not helped to stem the appalling havoc which this horrifying condition wreaks on such a large percentage of the population. A spectrum of suffering ranges from those who

merely suffer discomfort in a single joint through those who are prevented occasionally from working full-time by exacerbations of the disease up to completely crippled, helpless, grotesquely deformed, pain-stricken invalids. The toll of man-hours lost in industrial production in Great Britain alone is staggering, but it hardly gives testimony to the millions of sufferers who have little hope of effective treatment — let alone cure.

In giving out to the world the cause of this disease for the first time, I make no claims for having discovered it myself. Tribute for this must go to the English Master, Who has been so deeply concerned through the years for the plight of His own people and all those sufferers who live in temperate lands. The disease is caused by a virus and, therefore, like most diseases of viral origin, is extremely old.

The soil of the earth is grossly infected with many old diseases, some of which have not yet been inflicted on mankind since our history was recorded. Dying men have been buried in the soil of the earth for millions of years. Some ancient civilizations are buried deeply, and only through geographical cataclysms are the virus-crystals that decimated them brought to the surface. Epidemics then result. Not every race succumbs to every disease, nor do members of an affected race all succumb. Some are immune; others are susceptible. Susceptibility to rheumatoid arthritis is governed by numerous factors elaborated here, but basically those who have physical bodies tinged with Lemurian stock are more susceptible than others, all other conditions being equal.

The author now describes the causative factors as they exist in England. The portal of entry into the body is through the skin. In England this is usually through breaks in the skin of the fingers and the feet, especially in the clefts between the toes. The damp weather and general lack of care for the feet provide ideal conditions for athlete's foot (tinea pedis). The virus is spread around by domestic animals, and the dog is the main culprit. No other nation loves dogs more than the English. The dogs pass the rheumatoid arthritis virus to the master's fingers; the fingers pass the virus to towels, and a shared towel rubbed vigorously into the skin spreads the infection throughout the family. It is no wonder there is a familial tendency about the condition, especially if the dog is regarded as one of the family, as he usually is! Anyone who has kept dogs in cold climates will have noted how racked with rheumatic pain and stiffness they can become, especially in old age.

Infection and re-infection will go on indefinitely in this way. Exacerbations and effective treatment frequently coincide with two important factors: so-called rest, always recommendable with inflammatory conditions, especially when the patient goes to hospital or is confined to her room, which usually removes the main causative factor, at least temporarily, *i.e.*, the dog. The other important consideration is dry weather. Like the bacteria which produce gonorrhea, the rheumatoid arthritis virus needs moist and temperate conditions to be most effective. Sleeping in damp conditions, wet shoes, socks and other clothing all contribute to make entry of the virus easier, perhaps through the continually dampened skin becoming more permeable to them.

From the portal of entry in the skin, the virus passes down the lymphatic ducts into the blood stream, and after a considerable prodromal period lasting weeks or even months, the arthritis shows itself. It is during the prodromal period that the organism is establishing itself and, like all virus infections, the etheric or vital body suffers first. There is fatigue, malaise, weight loss, sweating especially in the hands and feet (thus vitiating the athlete's foot, if present), tachycardia, pains and stiffness.

There are alterations in the erythrocytes sedimentation rate.* This has significance in the conduct of treatment of rheumatoid arthritis.

A generalized infection develops and then one or more joints will be the target of attention; usually the finger joints suffer first. The joints become tender and swollen, while nodules may form nodule tendons of the wrists.

Karmic Factors
One asks what sort of karma has produced this chemical picture? Rigidity of thought, emotions, word and deed in past lives. The arthritis imposes such a burden of effort on the patient that he inevitably longs to be free (from his rigidity). This is helpful to the soul, and in the lives ahead concretised attitudes in the personality vehicle become undermined, and freer expression of the Soul results.

---

* See *Esoteric Healing, Part One,* p. 64.

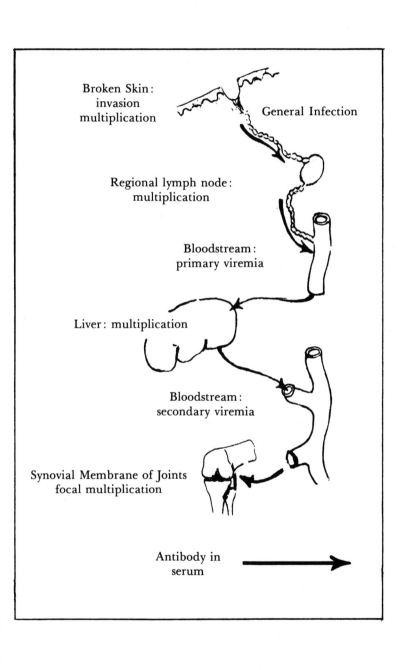

Broken Skin:
invasion
multiplication

General Infection

Regional lymph node:
multiplication

Bloodstream:
primary viremia

Liver: multiplication

Bloodstream:
secondary viremia

Synovial Membrane of Joints
focal multiplication

Antibody in
serum

Steroid Hormones versus Aspirin

In 1969 Hench and his colleagues reported dramatic improvement in patients suffering from rheumatoid arthritis who had been treated with cortisone. But the years have shown that the side-effects of this and other steroid hormones have outweighed the benefits of the therapy. Eminent bodies in Great Britain have shown through experimental research that the advantages of cortisone-like materials are not significantly better than those achieved by the common aspirin, and they have recommended the latter as the lesser of the two evils.

For reasons given in many parts of this book, endocrine glands are of special importance in reflecting the energies derived from the inner life of the patient via his chakras. Any gross interference with these glands (with certain exceptions from the point of view of the individual seen as a composite being of many vehicles) are a disaster and outweigh any purely physical effects. When given in effective doses, steroids depress the adrenal glands which are related to a variety of functions and, at the same time, to the Chakra at the Base of the Spine which *must* function in atom, plant, animal, Man and even Masters of the Wisdom.

Aspirin has side-effects which are more variable than steroids, but less obnoxious in general. They are the lesser of the two evils.

Drug Therapy

The majority of drugs claimed to have a specific effect in rheumatoid arthritis have proved valueless and have now been discarded.

Recommended Treatment

(1)   Counselling on the karmic nature of the disorder along the lines described above should bring out a more positive attitude, and this itself lends to treatment.

(2)   The general advice of the patient's medical doctor pertaining to the physical body parts and the curtailment of their mobility should be acted upon.

(3)   Removal of the cause of infection. This in itself will test the rigidness of the patient and the hold which karma has on him!

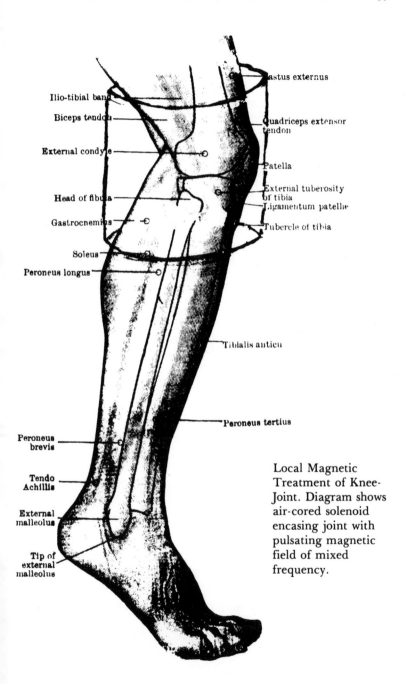

Ilio-tibial band

Biceps tendon

External condyle

Head of fibula

Gastrocnemius

Soleus

Peroneus longus

Peroneus
brevis

Tendo
Achillis

External
malleolus

Tip of
external
malleolus

Vastus externus

Quadriceps extensor
tendon

Patella

External tuberosity
of tibia

Ligamentum patellæ

Tubercle of tibia

Tibialis anticu

Peroneus tertius

Local Magnetic
Treatment of Knee-
Joint. Diagram shows
air-cored solenoid
encasing joint with
pulsating magnetic
field of mixed
frequency.

(4)   Prevention of reinfection through strict hygiene; the maintenance of a dry, warm environment or removal to more equable sunny climes.

(5)   A due consideration of the side-effects of aspirin should be made by the patient. He should weigh these against the ennobling effects which pain can bestow, and so long as no self-blame or guilt is allowed to arise, he should make his own choice.

(6)   Natural herbs should be used where possible. The writer, an Englishman, has known only mild arthritis in one ankle on rare occasions. In his garden there grows wild the extremely poisonous herb belladonna. He has taken this herb wild and rubbed its leaves into his ankle until only a green stain remained. Relief always comes and it is almost immediately. Possibly belladonna in creams or a salve can be obtained from a herbalist.

(7)   Magnetism. In earlier days when experimenting with pulsating magnetic fields, we noted that the sedimentation rate of the patient (E.S.R.) was lowered significantly when normal subjects were exposed to magnetic fields in our systemic treatment (see Appendix I). Later the same effect was produced on the greatly elevated E.S.R. of arthritic patients. As a lowering of the E.S.R. is taken to be an indication of effective treatment, we used this as a gauge in our treatment of arthritis with magnetic fields. Where there was a lowering of E.S.R., we were encouraged to proceed with treatment and, sure enough, reduction of swelling, increased mobility, and lessening of pain would follow. Alas, not all patients reponded in this way. Only too frequently a positive and cooperative attitude on the part of the patient indicated a good prognosis. Hence the importance of item (1) above. The general procedure for magnetic therapy was to give a systemic treatment twice a week for one hour. Then, little by little, local treatment was added. Solenoids were placed close to and even around affected parts.*

* See illustration on page 59 and Appendix I.

10

Mongolism: Assimilation of Soul Qualities

Recently two Pakistani doctors were discussing the incidence of mongolism in England. Both felt that this was on the increase and that in their own land, there was nothing like the incidence of the condition as found in England. This may be true. Patterson* puts it at one in 600 defectives held in institutions.

What esoteric implications are conveyed by the condition? Some have said that this genetic abnormality heralds a new subrace in the making; others feel that it acts as a warning against radio-active fallout. There is no truth in either of these propositions.

From tissue cultures of mongols' white cells, it has been found that chromosome No. 21 is triple in nature, instead of the usual duality. The extra chromosome, giving 47 instead of 46, arises by non-disjunction during germ cell formation. The incidence increases in the ova of older mothers. Because the span of fertility seems to be increasing, especially in Britain, this may account for the increase in Britain and the West. Many so-called schizophrenics may simply be older people and disciples who are experiencing increased levels of awareness.

The Karma, Parents and Child
The esotericist may say with certainty, however, that the condition is peculiarly karmic. Congenital heart conditions are the most karmic of all physical abberations, there being a most

* *Sick Children* by Donald Patterson, published by Cassell.

special affinity between the anatomy of the heart with its four
main cavities and the Four Great Lords of Karma. Mongolism
carries with it congenital heart disease in some 15 per cent of
the instances.

Both parents are involved in the karma. The nervous system
is also involved, with the brain being small, its cortex thinned
and its convolutions simple. The endocrine system is not
generally affected. In fact, ruled as it is by the Second Ray of
Love-Wisdom, it is not surprising to find that mongol children
are usually very lovable and affectionate, and the soul chooses
the most unaffected system through which to express itself:

'The soul is not where it lives but where it loves.'
                                              — H. G. Bohn

The Karma of Animal Grafts

I stress the endocrine system because some parents of mongol
children go to endless expense — exploring every conceivable
avenue of therapy in the hope of 'doing something' for the
child. Some never abandon the secret belief that the child can
be miraculously delivered of his abnormality. Some have even
had the expensive Niehans therapy, in which the eminent Swiss
doctor injects animal cells or grafts animal glands into his
patients. This may produce temporary rejuvenation for some,
but nothing can be done for the mongol whose endocrines are,
as already stated, quite normal. The karmic retribution for use
of animal grafts should dissuade unwary esotericists at least,
from resorting to this abomination in the eyes of the Lord of
Civilization.

The question arises: what to do for these youngsters? The
question of euthanasia does not even remotely suggest itself
here. Nor is there any likelihood of reproduction. What can be
done is to treat the child in such a way as to reduce the
hypotonicity of the muscles and joints and to bring the
constitution up to its maximum level of possible efficiency so
that the child may function more harmoniously in his
environment. With homoeopathic treatment some significant
improvement has been found in general alertness and an
increase in vocabulary over a period of six months has been
noted. But again, it must be stressed that treatment can only
be successful from the point of view of bringing the child to his
maximum functional capacity within the limits of his genetic
condition.

Treatment
Halibut Liver Oil, daily by capsule; homoeopathic dose: c.
Sodium Pentothal. Vitamin A administered antenatally to the
mother.

Very little can be done for the mongol child, and they rarely
reach adulthood. Any treatment that helps to integrate them
with their home, whether that be shared with their parents or
with other mongols in an institution is recommendable. The
use of music has been successful in bringing out some sort of
personality expression. The mongol child derives great
pleasure from music therapy, co-operates and responds to the
therapist and to other children.

This leads to greater independence without necessarily any
mental growth. Nor should the latter be expected. It is not in
the karma.

The Karma of Mongolism
The previous life of the mongol child was one in which there
was severe mental involvement in a variety of matters which
produced mental stress to the point of breakdown. There was
overloading of the nervous system and mental body . . . 'The
Fires of Mind consumed the physical tenure of the Soul', as
Browning put it. This demands, in the next life (or lives)
periods of enforced mental rest so that the various related
permanent atoms of the mental, emotional and physical
vehicles have time to assimilate, co-ordinate and effectively
'digest', store, file and integrate the lessons learnt from the life
of excessive mental pre-occupation.

Life as a mongol removes all possible chance of mental
stress, processing or stimulation. The rest is enforced. Mongol
children are loving but not mental; pleasure-seeking but not
capable of moralising. We should remember the karmic factors
involved and help the young soul through its period of 'physical'
convalescence after its brutal experiences in a mentally
polarized and stressful series of lives.

11

Alcoholism: A Thirst for Power

Origin of Alcholism
Man began drinking alcohol very early on this planet, certainly before Atlantis. Thus, in Lemuria, it was used mainly as a device for stimulating the body's mechanisms for adjusting to changes in outside temperature. Earliest man's homoeostasis devices were immature. His skin was very thin and had not yet developed that richness of organelles by which it is now characterized. Its insulatory devices (*e.g.* subcutaneous fat) and its blood capillary shunts were poorly established and had to await the sympathetic nervous system and its coordination with the fast maturing central nervous system. Sensory organs for deferring and adjusting to heat and cold were disseminated very late in the skin, and this need was met in earliest men by the pineal gland acting on the hypothalamic regions of the brain.

The thickening of the skin, its keratinization to prevent water loss, its incorporation of tactile and other organs of sensation came very late. Yeast cells had always flourished, deriving as they do from the plant kingdom and given a spirit, as they were by the advent of the angiosperms and their fruit-bearing trees about eighty million years ago. About that time, Man (mainly those elements individualizing on the Moon Chain) began to materialize the first elements of his physical structures.

The ecstatic and etheric states of consciousness experienced during man's habitation of the Hyperborean Continent* were progressively lost during his transition from a purely etheric being into one with an etherico-physical vehicle. He fed, at first, on juices and fruits, and these, when accumulated and allowed to ferment, gave him an exhilaratory beverage which, in addition, provided him with semblances of his long lost but instinctual memories of ecstatic states in Hyperborea, where spiritual beings were almost as common as primitive ones. They associated the two and our present word 'spirits' for alcohol is testimony of this, the 'gift of the gods'. This has an important bearing on what follows herein. It is perhaps too much to suppose that in addition to the ordinary interpretation of the derivation of the word 'alcohol' (of Arabic origin), 'hol' once referred to the drinker being made 'whole' — hence 'holism' or one with the gods, imbued with his lost nature, *i.e.*, spirit. Nevertheless, to the primitive men, this is what drinking the beverage implied.

Much later, as Man began to develop his Solar Plexus Chakra and, with it, his emotional nature — a spiritual event for him at that stage of his development — emotional growth was stimulated by alcohol, reinforcing the concept of the beverage's spiritual qualities. Today, for Man on the Path, orientation away from emotional license into mental polarity is the order of spiritual things, and alcohol, though it may bring vague surfacings of archetypal memories of past spiritual glories, is not in any way an adjunct to or a passport for spiritual advance.

Nevertheless, in the earliest days, alcohol was prepared by the priests and medicine men, and its imbibition was always in ceremonial groups accompanied by appropriate rituals, invocation and incantations led by the appropriate tribal officials. Minstrels and reciting bards were meant to bring back memories of former glories. Dancing by maids and youths reminded the more mature of the lost land between lives wherein physical imperfections imposed by age held no sway.

Drinking or toasting by warriors before and after a battle not only reinforced unity and gave the event dramatic overtones, but made good sense in terms of 'Dutch' courage. Without casting any aspersions on the courage of comrades in arms in the Western Desert during the Second World War, all would agree that the trucks of Palestinian wine or brandy were a

* See *Anthropogeny The Esoteric Origin of Man* by the present writer.

welcome sight during the long periods of abysmal defeat before
final victory in the Desert, and commanders, even under
puritan-like Montgomery of Alemain, made sure they were
given every opportunity to reach the war front.

After the war, there were brave attempts at maintaining a
transient comradery through reunions reinforced with alcoholic
excesses, but these were pale candles in the suns of wartime
associations, and reunions of college classes and 'Old Boys'
gatherings are no better. But they do illustrate the powerful
persistence of an ancient tradition that elevated experiences
are best cemented when accompanied by alcoholic intoxication.

In Greece, and later in Rome, orgies of drinking accompanied
the rituals of the religious cults of Dionysus and Bacchus.
These were by no means haphazard and pointless events. The
Master Robert Browning indicates that the use of the product
of the vine in these sects symbolized, in drunkenness, that
esoteric knowledge that the Earth was tilted on its axis and that
its motion occasionally wobbled. It is only recently that his
knowledge has been shown to have had any significance. The
occurence of ice ages, their extent and their time periods are
related to these factors. Also, through drunkenness in others,
the initiate was shown what lack of control looked like and to
guard against loss of balance, harmony and control was to put
them to test under the impact of alcohol. We shall observe the
relevance of this information to our subject in due course.

The Dionysian cults were well aware that alcohol promoted
this abreaction so precious and desirous to the disciple. It is
worth considering the matter in some detail in order to
understand the esoteric aspects of alcoholism.

An Atlantean Disorder

There is no doubt about alcoholism being a condition of
weakness inherited from Atlantis. Groups of Atlantean souls
are coming into incarnation together, and part of their mission
is to reduce the karma of that great cosmic entity Who is using
the Atlantean Root Race as his physical body of expression.
Many of us have physical bodies of Atlantean stock susceptible
still to Atlantean disorders. The impact of stress in our present
society brings out and shows up these Atlantean weaknesses.

The Alchemy of Alcohol

Alcohol is chemically related to water through its hydroxyl

(OH) group of atoms. Water, or H_2O, is better read as HOH and is technically 'hydroalcohol'. Like water, alcohol has some astounding and unique properties, and like water, large amounts of it are absorbed through the wall of the stomach directly into the blood. Oxygen on its own can also be absorbed by the newborn child through the wall of the gastric mucosa. Indeed, when infant Man was still grappling with the problems of oxygenation thirty billion years ago, his stomach held him in good stead as an accessory lung as well as an absorber of glucose juices and their ferments, long before the digestion of solid vegetables and fruits necessitated the lengthening of the intestine and its morphological diversification.

Ecstasy, as it is understood by esoteric science, results from sudden movements and influxes of energy in the etheric body and its aura. Alcohol provides the physical body with boosts of high calorific energy. It is a food, but a food that has almost twice the calorific value of carbohydrates and protein. Only fats exceed it in this respect. But it is through its actions on the movement of blood and, indirectly, the propulsion of prana throughout the brain and nervous system that it consoles man, and it is through its removal of inhibitions that it exuberates him.

Alcohol moderates the critical faculties of the brain and removes the vagal nerve action of slowing down the heart rate. It becomes an instrument of maya, part of the grand illusion that snares all men. It brings the effects of maya right down into the body cells. We *feel* better for it and, therefore, think we are better for it. The desires for new experience, response and security are all given freer rein but most especially the desire for recognition. It is a false elixir, a spurious philosopher's stone: 'the subtle alchemist that in a trice Life's leaden metal into gold transmute.'

The euphoria that alcohol provides comes from believing you are better than you are when, in fact, at least from the psychological viewpoint, you are becoming less and less competent in a huge range of faculties. No wonder neophytes of Dionysus and Bacchus were introduced to alcohol debauches and then, later, as sober novitiates, were shown from behind curtains the same revels — to illustrate with sad emphasis what lack of control can do to the minds and actions of men, the implication being that all men are, to an extent, subject to maya and intoxicated by the material world.

Alcohol deadens the mind to mental pain and the body to physical suffering. The emotions are given freer license, but at the expense of the hard won gifts of refinement, poise and purpose. Vision and memory are impaired, the performance of the muscular system is lowered, and centres of the brain progressively shut down.

Blood Concentration of Alcohol

A.   100mg per 100ml equals dizzy and delightful.
B.   200mg per 100ml equals drunk and disorderly.
C.   300mg per 100ml equals dead drunk.
D.   400mg per 100ml equals death's door (respiratory paralysis)

The deadening of the body by alcohol to the effects of pain is the first indication that the etheric matrix is becoming 'thinned out', if not actually detached from the physical body. Not only is diminishing judgement impairing the efficiency of the body functions, but there is literally less vital energy being made available to the physical organs, the muscles, nerves, etc.

Paradoxically, the resulting condition allows the astral body to act almost directly upon the physical shell. Emotions are almost uninhibited. The alcohol has a grossening effect and, speaking esoterically, this means that the astral body gets closer to the objects of its desires. In fact, during the episode of drunkenness, the astral body becomes completely aligned with the physical body; even during sleep or alcoholic coma, it cannot separate itself. We will note the importance of this phenomenon later.

Health Hazards of Alcohol

The burden of detoxification of the alcohol and its elimination is almost entirely placed on the liver, which can dispose of about one ounce of alcohol per hour. Little or no alcohol is excreted by the kidneys and lungs. This places a heavy load on the liver and, what is more important, on the Solar Plexus Chakra, a centre that is already stimulated and out of control in most of humanity. •

It is true to say that alcohol is a food of a high energy level which is completely without vitamins. But it is not true to say that the liver will not degenerate if the alcoholic eats enough other food containing a sufficiency of vitamins. The truth is that recent scientific evidence shows that alcohol affects every cell that it comes into contact with.* This finding is quiet confirmation of an esoteric teaching of long standing that alcohol is a general poison, especially for Man on the Path.

C. W. Leadbeater, the great theosophical clairvoyant of the early part of this century, could observe, clairvoyantly, the effects of alcohol on the body and taught (eighty years ago) that its effects were those of a general poison. It was also he who taught that cigarette smoking was a health hazard, sixty years before the Royal College of Physicians issued the first official announcement that there was a correlation between cigarette smoking and lung cancer. Leadbeater also observed the precincts of drinking houses from the level of the astral plane and the effects of astral forces and entities on alcoholic imbibers.**

Alcohol and its Effects

The author was able to review the effects of alcohol on himself in the immediate post-war period. Even the light use of alcohol had to be abandoned when he began to tread the Path some thirty years ago or restricted to an occasional glass of table wine. Understanding alcohol's many effects with the help of his medical knowledge, as well as his esoteric understanding, he makes the following comments which may be of help:

(1) With even the mildest alcoholic consumption, there is inflammation of the gastro-intestinal tract, causing pain and diarrhoea.

(2) Acidosis, malaise* and nausea with a pounding headache.

(3) An exhaustion lasting as long as two days. The most distressing aspect of this is the loss of the creative faculty, felt as a sort of spiritual aridity as if the Soul had momentarily fled.

---

* *Scientific American*, March 1976.
** *Occult Chemistry* by C. W. Leadbeater and Annie Besant.
* Discomfort, uneasiness and indisposition.

(4) Increased activity of the brow area, with auric sensations (similar to the period that precedes a migraine attack). Occasionally this period might bring on high spiritual experiences, often with symbols strongly relevant to the preceding twenty-four hours.

(5) Vivid dreams, especially before waking and of the 'warning' type; dreams filled with symbols of impending disaster.

(6) Insomnia. A period of four hours heavy sleep after drinking, and then an insomnia that heralded in the first symptoms of hangover.

(7) A disgust welling up from a deep level of consciousness.

(8) An exacerbation of hypoglycaemia attacks (discovered during early years of medical training).

These, on their own, would be sufficient to accentuate the sensitivity of the alcoholic to inner experiences. When there is also instability of personality, the hypoglycaemia can enduce schizophrenic and paranoic outburts.

(9) With the disgust, there came a catharsis — a surfacing of elements of the Dweller on the Threshold* at a time when the psyche is least ready and able to deal with them.

Esoteric Aspects of Alcoholism

It is well known that when a man treads the Path, all that is good and all that is evil rises in him, so that he is forced into a mighty confrontation with those elements of his nature. Those which are involutionary constitute the components of his 'dweller'. Those which are evolutionary, or good, constitute fragments of his fast-coalescing 'Angel of the Shining Presence', guardian of the door (for him) of initiation.

---

* See also *Jewel In The Lotus*, 155-159; *Meditation*, 268, 288; and *Psychology Of Discipleship*, 15-20, 65-67, 231, all by the present writer.

It will help the healer to review some of the problems encountered by the disciple in dealing with mental and emotional disorders of the lower triad in a process known as abreaction.

With his increased sensitivity, with his greater strength and with purpose and direction clear in his mind, the disciple accepts the challenge presented not only by surfacing memories and experiences in this life, but of previous lives, which together have formed his present dweller on the threshold of the consciousness at this early stage of his discipleship. The dweller is a loathsome entity; its components are astral matter of the lowest orders. It preys on the neophyte, drawing its substance from him during times of fear, worry, horror and other negative thinking during which the astral body (not yet integrated) haemorrhages. The dweller forms a negative vortex in a force field of which the chela is the positive and donating pole. The dispatch of this entity comes when it is confronted and recognized for what it is. The flow of auric energies towards it ceases, and from sheer strangulation it flags and withers. But it is an entity and will fight back for its survival, taking every opportunity to highlight any negative scene or emotion with its presence just at a time when the disciple is shifting his focus from the outer world to the inner. It is finally replaced with the birth and steady growth of the 'Angel of the Shining Presence', representing structures in Atma, Buddhi and Manas being progressively built into the aura through the assiduous efforts of the disciple in meditation and through his services to mankind and his devotion to the study of the occult classics. This is the background for the would-be-initiate. It involves the replacement of old codes of conduct, preconceived or established ideas that tyrannized the mind of the disciple from his earliest years and which have been consolidated by his religion and his education. The individual's dweller is but part of the gigantic Dweller on the Threshold of awareness of MANKIND. He draws from the collective phobias, idiosyncracies and thoughtforms of mankind. In destroying his own dweller, he performs an act of service to mankind for, in so doing, he has also reduced the potency of that huge planetary entity anchored to the lowest planes of the astral world. This dweller is part of the collective unconscious described by Professor Carl Jung.*

---

* *Psychology Of Discipleship*, 15-17, by the present writer.

Dr Francis Merchant gives a fine exposition of the more esoteric aspects of the Dionysian philosophy as practised in Greece.*

This small country has given the world a multitude of highly significant myths. Prometheus, Jason, Hercules, Theseus, Oedipus — all these names arouse meaningful associations. There is one Greek divinity, however, who is rather infrequently discussed although his symbol is greatly honoured in modern society. I speak of Dionysus, who is commonly known as Bacchus, the god of wine. His modern followers seem to know little of the god to whom they pay homage.

Only a few stray incidents about Dionysus have come down to us. He was the son of Jupiter; the wine and the corn were sacred to him. Those who participated in the rites he instituted attained through ecstasy a sense of oneness with divinity. King Midas is also associated with this god. Having befriended Dionysus, the King was told to ask for anything he wanted. He expressed the wish that everything he touched might be turned into gold. The granting of his request brought Midas no happiness, for his very food became inedible.

Sailors who sought to sell Dionysus into slavery were turned into Dolphins. King Pentheus, who prohibited the celebration of Dionysian rites, perished in consequence of his opposition.

We are told that the Greek drama arose out of the Dionysian festivals. In the Eleusinian Mysteries, Dionysus played an important role.

Wine, money and dramatic conflict — enduring symbols through the centuries — are thus emphasized by these myths.

The intoxication of the grape is but a symbol of the bliss attending spiritual union. The physical exhilaration that comes from imbibing wine is but an anticipatory of the exaltation inspired by creative ideas.

Dionysus stands for the inrush of inspirational energy that breaks up established modes and patterns. Physical intoxication, like sex, is but the lowest rung of the great mystery. Expansion and union have different meanings at various points of the ascending spiral of consciousness. The intoxication of the soul is to that of the body what fire is to the shadow it casts.

Those who cannot resolve their conflicts at the level of the soul seek relief in the negative unity that resides in the forgetfulness of drink.

---

* *The Gold Hoard* by Francis Mercant, pp. 253-254.

The heart of the drama is conflict — conflict that springs from man's sense of duality, of separativeness, of disjunction. Endlessly he suffers, ever seeking the resolution of his dissonance. In sex he seeks union; in drink, expansion. Dionysus points to higher techniques for achieving a more refined expression of these impelling tendencies. Union with the soul and the expansion of consciousness resulting from self-forgetfulness are gifts of Dionysus that have not yet been generally accepted. In the drama we have man's attempt to objectify his conflicts in order that he might attain to understanding. The rapture of the poet and the mystic is an expression of intoxication at a higher level of awareness.

King Midas, his mind centered on gold, could profit nothing from the god's bounty — nor can the King's modern successors.

The rites of Dionysus, it has been said, are still being performed today. His body — the corn — is eaten, and his blood — the vine — is drunk. The participants in the ritual, however, often know naught of the god they honor, nor of the spiritual correspondences to which the external symbols point.

Spiritus — Union or Poison?

It has been said that the thirst for alcohol is merely an outward manifestation of an inner urge for spiritual union. To support this, Carl Jung pointed out that the latin word for alcohol is 'spiritus' and that it is identical with the same work in latin used for the higher religious experience. Perhaps Professor Jung's letter needs to be quoted in full:

I had no news from Roland H. any more and often wondered what has been his fate. Our conversation which he has adequately reported to you had an aspect of which he did not know. The reason that I could not tell him everything was that those days I had to be exceedingly careful of what I said. I had found out that I was misunderstood in every possible way. Thus I was very careful when I talked to Roland H. But what I really thought about was the result of many experiences with men of his kind.

His craving for alcohol was the equivalent, on a low level, of the spiritual thirst of our being for wholeness, expressed in medieval language: the union with God.*

How could one formulate such an insight in a language that is not misunderstood in our days?

The only right and legitimate way to such an experience is that it happens to you in reality, and it can only happen to you when

* 'As the hart panteth after the water brooks, so panteth my soul after Thee, O God.' (Psalm 42:1)

you walk on a path which leads you to higher understanding. You might be led to that goal by an act of grace or through a personal and honest contact with friends, or through a higher education of the mind beyond the confines of mere rationalism. I see from your letter that Roland H. has chosen the second way, which was, under the circumstances, the best one.

I am strongly convinced that the evil principle prevailing in this world leads the unrecognized spiritual need into perdition if it is not counteracted either by real religious insight or by the protective wall of human community. An ordinary man, not protected by an action from above and isolated in society, cannot resist the power of evil, which is called very aptly the Devil. But the use of such words arouses so many mistakes that one can only keep aloof from them as much as possible.

These are the reasons why I could not give a full and sufficient explanation to Roland H., but I am risking it with you because I conclude from your very decent and honest letter that you have acquired a point of view above the misleading platitudes one usually hears about alcoholism.

You see, 'alcohol' in Latin is SPIRITUS, and you use the same word for the highest religious experience as well as for the most depraving poison. The helpful formula therefore is: SPIRITUS CONTRA SPIRITUM. . . .*

If this were entirely true of alcoholics, it would explain how the condition seems to develop inexorably where the life style, the marriage, the occupation, the cultural pursuits, etc., do not allow the expression of the soul. The inflow of the spiritual waters is inhibited because there is no outflow for them, or where there is an inability to express them in an environment that is stifling and arid.

It does not mean that the alcoholic is uncreative; many are extremely so, but whether their soul's purpose is being expressed in their creativeness is another matter.

The Karma of Alcoholism — The Need for Attention

All individuals, somewhere in some life, have had to face the problem of alcoholism — have been tested with it and found wanting. There is no field of human experience in which the monad will not plunge his lower triad — for it is in *overcoming* every aspect of material enmeshment that the monad gains spiritual staying power.

* *The Grapevine*, International Monthly Journal of Alcoholics Anonymous, Vol. 24, No. 8, January 1968.

The drives of many individuals are so varied and intense that the call of the Soul, the voice of conscience, cannot be heard. When these circumstances continue life after life, the Soul may choose a life in which all the drives are focused into one overweening and all-consuming desire, *i.e.*, for alcohol. This concentration of a host of spread-eagled drives into one makes the Soul's task easier. It reduces the number of lives needed to break the hold which the glamour of sensory and material matters have on its lower triad.

In previous lives, the alcoholic has held high-ranking positions in society. There, he has been the cynosure of all eyes, praised, adored, even hero-worshipped. But he abused his position. Instead of providing an example — a leader to his people — he became englamoured. He was too distracted by his own station, its dramatic appeal, by the sensory thrills it provided, the security and the elevation of stature. He failed to put his rank and position to good effect, ignored the sufferings of the masses, the appeals of the weak and voiceless. Instead, there developed a thirst for power, almost a megalomania.

It has been said there is one law for man and another law for the very beautiful. Like many beautiful people, these englamoured leaders abused the law and later are faced with the karma of their actions. Many beautiful people use the law justly and wisely; others abuse it. It is so very true of this karmic group — powerful people who abused their high stations and have to pay for that corruption in later lives as alcoholics. But why as alcoholics?

In this life, the alcoholic becomes again the focus of attention, but now it is for different reasons. Now he is the cynosure of all eyes because of his debasement of himself. He becomes a mark for ridicule, disgust and scorn. In his intoxicated state, he often acts out his elevated and pretentious opinions of himself, his megalomania, his grandiose schemes and attitudes. But now no one is fooled by such charades. The pendulum has swung to its opposite. 'Vengeance is mine; I will repay, saith the Lord.'

Karmic Results

There are as many karmic results of alcoholism as there are misdemeanours committed under its influence. Perhaps the most relevant to our times is the karma of drunken driving. I asked the Master Robert Browning to give me a visual image of the karma that results from the irresponsible actions of a driver that drinks without any regard for those who might be menaced by his resulting incapability. As always, in such visual impressions flashed from the mind of the Master, you yourself must play the central figure — not a very encouraging experience when you are asking for visual impressions during occult research into the causes of such illnesses as rheumatoid arthritis and cancer. In the vision that follows, I had to play the central figure, the dramatic 'I':

> I was standing on a hillside looking towards my left at a freeway in the distance. A group of children were standing on the curbside, wanting to cross the road. They correctly looked towards their right and then to the left to make sure no vehicles were coming, then held each other's hands and began to move quickly across the highway. Suddenly an automobile appeared over the brow of the hill and approached the group of children at break-neck speed. Terrified they scattered, but to no avail. The car bore down and ploughed into them. I was horrified.
>
> The scene faded and then resumed. Now, there was the sound of a train's whistle in the distance. I looked over to the right and saw there was a great curve in the railway line down in the valley. From the curve, the line crossed a bridge. I could see that the train was travelling much too fast to take the curve. The engine driver was drunk. The train plunged over the edge of the curve into the deep ravine below. Screams from the trapped and dying reached me. I ran down towards the wreckage. The carnage was awful. Between the dust and smoke I could see men tearing at the wreckage; the critically injured lay everywhere.
>
> Suddenly everything went silent, and in the awful hush, I found that everyone was staring at me. I stopped in my tracks and cried, 'What's the matter?' There was a pause, and then someone faltered, 'You are the only doctor here. You must take charge.' I was stunned. I had no drugs, no surgical instruments . . . nothing. The responsibility of my position was appalling. I was the cynosure of all eyes. I was crushed by the weight of my circumstances as men and women and even trapped children cried to me for help.

This is the karma that results from drunken driving. In lives to come, such transgressors will be faced with situations of tremendous responsibility — responsibilities beyond their means, in which they will be given the opportunity to 'work off' the karma of irresponsibility which they evoked during their episodes of drunken driving in the earlier life.

Therapeutic Effects of Responsibility

It is hard to suggest that the shouldering of responsibility be a part of the therapy for rehabilitated alcoholics. Heaven knows they have enough to contend with as it is. But where there is esoteric understanding, where spiritual strength is returning, part of the rehabilitation should be to shoulder responsibilities for mankind beyond that which normally faces a sensitive being. In simple words, the best therapy of all should lead to discipline, to concern for the welfare of others, to sharing responsibility for the planet. This is the way of the disciple.

But, of course, this is exactly what Alcoholics Anonymous asks: that those who are rehabilitated help those who are still struggling.

The Factor of Love

Apart from the karmic factors already presented, there is a very basic underlying weakness in alcoholics. It is more of a blockage of energy than lack of it. The alcoholic needs love and needs to manifest love.

He must be taught, not selfish, attaching love, but selfless love. Not an 'I-will-love-you-if-you-will-love-me-back' attitude, but an 'I-will-love-you-no-matter-what'.

Discrimination of the Real from the unreal, the assumption of responsibilities for others, the practice of compassion for all living things, these are the disciplines which could reduce the tremendous build-up of energies around the Solar Plexus Chakra of the alcoholic. If he himself cannot evoke these qualities within him, then the esoteric healer should apply them to the alcoholic. The stimulation of his heart region will ease the strains for him and loosen the grasp of possessive entities.

Psychotherapeutic Treatment

The alcoholic lacks the power to transfer energies from the Solar Plexus Chakra, which lies below the diaphragm, into the Heart Chakra which lies above the diaphragm. Its energies are almost entirely emotional and attaching. Thwarted emotionally in his daily affairs, his attachments quickly centre on that which he can hold firmly in his hands and which will substitute for him things that will replace the series of broken images, idols he had erected for himself to worship at and which life had so rudely destroyed.

The great Master of the Wisdom and Lord of Compassion, K.H., who in his previous life was St Francis of Assisi, used these words:

> God grant me the serenity to accept the things I cannot change;
> The courage to change the things I can,
> And the wisdom to know the difference.

They have been adopted as the Serenity Prayer of Alcoholics Anonymous.

It is easy to understand why Alcoholics Anonymous is so successful. It incorporates so many aspects of the Ray of Love-Wisdom: its universality, its compassion, its service to mankind, etc. The esoteric student and healer would do well to ponder on its aims and method:

(1) Belief in God and *Natural Law*...compare this with Karma.

(2) Frank *self-appraisal*...meditation uses the same techniques.

(3) Willingness to admit and correct wrongs done to others...facing the Karma of *this* life.

(4) A trust in Mankind...concept of Universal Brotherhood.

(5) Dedication to rescue those who sincerely desire to conquer alcoholism by making them members as successful abstainers...'Am I my brother's keeper?' To the esotericist, the answer is 'Yes!'

Group Psychotherapy
AA's system of psychotherapy has rehabilitated more alcoholics than the combined resources of medicine, psychology and psychiatry. Motivated by the survival needs of its members rather than by the scientific curiosity of orthodox medicine or the blind discipline of a doctor-patient relationship, its greatest value lies in its group therapy treatment of the problem of alcoholism. A minority movement, seeking justice in a world that classes the alcoholic as deviant and immoral, AA gives the alcoholic what he has always wanted — social acceptance by a

group that cares about him and understands him, especially at his lowest.

The outstanding characteristics of the alcoholic at his lowest are:

Wrong motivation...everything is sacrificed for the binge.

Separativeness...he will drink alone, endlessly, and be hostile to non-alcoholics.

Indifference, harmfulness, selfishness, ingratitude.

All these are the very opposite manifestations of Love-Wisdom. The least the therapist can do is to prescribe Flower Remedies for these symptoms. In taking a case history before prescribing, the list given above (by no means complete) should aid the gentle enquiries of the therapist.

As we review the levels of disintegration which the alcoholic patient goes through on his downward journey to his 'pit of hell', we are confronted with the soul condition, the mental condition, the astral condition, the etheric condition and finally the physical level of his symptomatic list. Beginning with the process of unnamed fear, the Flower Remedy prescribed will be ASPEN — for the person trembling with fright, especially a nameless fear, as most alcoholics will reveal, or even conceal, according to their temperaments.

Also give the patient AGRIMONY for his craving for alcohol. The first condition of treatment is to stop the intake of alcohol completely, and AGRIMONY can help him in this most desperate struggle.

Soul	HOLLY SWEET CHESTNUT
Mental	HORNBEAM (OLIVE) OAK (AGRIMONY)
Astral	CRAB APPLE GENTIAN
Etheric	OLIVE
Physical	ASPEN AGRIMONY

Emotionally, the patient will need the therapist's support —
something to help rid that deep feeling of self-disgust, as if he
wants to cleanse himself. Every human being at some time or
the other has had experiences at a physical level when getting
into a bath couldn't be quick enough (even airplane journeys,
crowded trains and buses can create such a desire). CRAB
APPLE is the Flower Remedy to dispose of the feelings of guilt
and disgust.

Then there is the etheric stage for the patient, the state of
physical exhaustion when his very life's blood seems to be
drained from him, when nothing vital is coming through the
etheric matrix; the prana just cannot get through. OLIVE is
the Remedy for this physical exhaustion on the etheric level of
his upswing.

Then, for the despair, doubts and depression which will
invade the patient from the astral plane to undermine all his
efforts toward rehabilitation, give him GENTIAN.

Then comes the mental level for consideration, where the
negative conditions listed above will all be present in the case
history. It is here that the therapist must begin to think of
prescribing by a repertoire of remedies, i.e., a whole series, for
mental symptoms are changeable in an individual, and the
changes are usually very frequent, especially in the alcoholic
patient. OLIVE for mental fatigue, AGRIMONY for the mental
torture, and HORNBEAM for sustained mental effort. It is here
that OAK will assist the patient in his struggle against mental
odds — the sort of odds that most alcoholics have to face when
people around them say, 'Oh, yes, we've heard all this before',
when he is desperately in need of their loving understanding.

At the soul level, at least six months after recovery, HOLLY
is the recipe for Love-Wisdom, and SWEET CHESTNUT for
anything related to the soul, e.g., the 'dark night of the soul'.
This brings the alcoholic back to the level where it all began —
his soul's desperate cry for recognition and expression.

Now, at last, there is real hope for him. He is sustained by
the combined strength of his group's aura, assisted by the
miraculous work of the simple, but powerful, Flower Remedies
prescribed for him as an individual and not for his condition.
Finally there is therapy available from the level of understanding
which may gain social acceptance, if not of the alcoholic
himself, at least of the real causes behind alcoholism.

12

Schizophrenia

Causes

Schizophrenia is described as an inherited predisposition to psychological dysfunction. This predisposition to manifest abnormal psychological behaviour can be activated, brought to the surface, by stress. The kind of physical body the schizophrenic has inherited in terms of nervous system and endocrine glands, the astral body which he has built in childhood and adolescence under the impact of his social environment, and the mental body which he has elaborated, all play their part in emphasizing or minimizing the expression of the dis-ease of the Soul with its vehicles. Where points of friction occur between the former and the latter, schizophrenic behaviour may manifest.

Many causes have been offered by investigators and clinicians since schizophrenia was first identified under the name of 'Dementia Praecox'. It presents itself frequently in childhood and there is high familial incidence. But there is no firm evidence of it being genetic.

However, the English Master maintains that this is so. There is a physical basis for the condition. It is linked to hidden genes which are recessive. When parents each bearing a recessive gene for schizophrenia are brought together, the child inherits a physical predisposition to schizophrenia. This may not show itself in signs and symptoms that warrant medical attention unless there are predisposing factors in the environment, like stress.

Which chromosome? This must wait for later research. Already the chromosomes are being mapped. Assistance in this work will come from the English Master in the near future, but the time is not yet.

The instability of relationships between the astral body and the mental body are exaggerated when certain genetic factors are present in the schizophrenic. This was commented upon, in different language, by Stransky, who in 1904 found not only inhibition of emotional expression, but dissociation and incoordination between the emotional and mental processes of the mind. In esoteric parlance, the condition is opposite to what is called an 'integrated personality', where there is blending of the mental and emotional nature under the hegemony and direction of the Personality Body. The emotional nature is there, but it is disciplined and refined: the thought processes are under control and are directed wilfully into channels that permit expression of the Soul's Purpose... I am THAT.

In Man *not* on the Path, the dictates of the Personality are important. The Emotional and Mental bodies are associated with personality drives and intentions... I am. In very unintegrated individuals, the personality is weak and they become the willing tool of whatever thoughts are elaborated by the Mental Body or emotions surfacing from the Astral Body.

In schizophrenia, the connexions between the personality and its vehicles become tenuous. There is disorder of association. Trains of thought take unusual paths away from the hegemony of the personality which, already lacking synthesis, becomes further weakened. Illogical thinking and incoherence in the Mental Body and its parts occur, and this situation allows categories and complexes of thought to become independent and isolated from the personality. It may now be understood why the symbol for this condition, in the English Ashram, is a bouncing rugby ball — its direction is unpredictable. Then these complexes become easily charged with emotional energy and oust the dominance of the personality altogether. The personality has no alternative but to fragment, to become a loose association of complexes — the opposite of the integrated personality.

Reality in terms of the personality no longer exists. The schizophrenic may not even see, much less comprehend, the world which used to surround his personality. He sees now everything in terms of his little 'I's' or energized complexes. Their fears and wishes become paramount and may take the form of symbols. Out of their exaggerated importance (to the detriment of any central personality that remains) come delusions.

Disorders in the Form of Thought

All schizophrenics show this if their condition persists long enough. This disorder results from a lack of purpose, a central theme around which the thoughts can build themselves into a cohesive and meaningful concept. It is manifest in everyone to some degree. A business tycoon may disagree. He would emphasize that he has a central purpose in what he does, but in terms of his Soul's Purpose, his activities may be meaningless or just a repetition of activities conducted in past lives.

In the schizophrenic, lacking purpose, even at a personality level, the condition shows as a sequence of thoughts whose direction may be altered by any intrusion into his consciousness, rather than holding to a steady course by a central determining idea. The thoughts, as they unfold, may be swerved by what he momentarily hears, or feels, or intuits and are carried hither and thither. There is always something in common between his thoughts, but they are unrelated to a central motive, purpose or idea. Thus, to the observer they would be meaningless because the connection between the thoughts is elaborated as the thoughts proceed and is not related to a central theme, idea or purpose.

At a different level we get groups of thoughts or ideas leading nowhere... *flights of ideas* and for some people, when these are written down, they can be even more disordered than when spoken.

One of the greatest names in modern English literature in the field of the novel is Virginia Woolf. She had a genius for describing the flow of human thought. Her novels are classics of introspection in a style that has never been copied, let alone equalled. Yet, who is there that has made a careful study of her novels and schizophrenia who cannot help noting how genius and madness are close akin:

It was at Bourton that summer, early in the nineties, when he was so passionately in love with Clarissa. There were a great many people there, laughing and talking, sitting round a table after tea,

DOOR BANGS

CURTAIN
DRAWS

Disordered Form of Thought

As compared with:

Thoughts about a Central Idea

THE FORMS OF THOUGHT

and the room was bathed in yellow light and full of cigarette smoke. They were talking about a man who had married his housemaid, one of the neighbouring squires, he had forgotten his name. He had married his housemaid and she had been brought to Bourton to call — an awful visit it had been. She was absurdly overdressed, 'like a cockatoo', Clarissa had said, imitating her, and she never stopped talking. On and on she went, on and on. Clarissa imitated her. Then somebody said — Sally Seton it was — did it make any real different to one's feelings to know that before they'd married she had had a baby? (In those days, in mixed company, it was a bold thing to say.) He could see Clarissa now, turning bright pink; somehow contracting; and saying, 'Oh, I shall never be able to speak to her again!' Whereupon the whole party sitting round the tea-table seemed to wobble. It was very uncomfortable.*

In this thought disorder, the individual is unable to confine himself to the business in hand, to focus his mind on the given topic. He seizes on any of the thought objects coming into his mind and may elaborate on them or become over-concerned with some quite superficial quality of an object that confronts his gaze. He isolates himself in doing this from the rest of his nervous system and because 'energy follows thought', his focus of attention to the object or scene before him becomes energized. It engrosses him. He becomes the dramatic 'I' in it. This isolation may continue so that he is eternally being diverted away from the mainstream of matters concerning the rest of himself, into backwaters. Thus, the schizophrenic's symptoms show lack of ability to concentrate, increased rigidity and distraction from intellectual performance. His isolating tendencies fix him on any stimulus that presents itself, and he responds excessively to them, adopts the centre of that scene and acts out its ramifications, giving what has sometimes been called the split personality — the ability to divorce himself from one set of circumstances to become the central dramatic 'I' in another.**

*   *Mrs Dalloway.*
** *Meditation, The Theory And Practice*, p. 137, by the present writer.

He may do this with sudden and great rapidity, especially when stress or crises make the normal personality untenable. The Master R.B. gave this visual symbol for the way in which this transference of attention of the schizophrenic from one personality to another was evoked:

> You are in a tank battle: your own vehicle becomes a main target. Shot after shot pounds the hull. One penetrates and kills the crew. The enemy are closing in. Another shot sets the tank on fire. You peer through the periscope at the battle. You note the green trees of the forest nearby. There is no other recourse; you must flee. You hurl open the turret cover and dash from the blazing inferno. Now you are free and amongst the trees. Here you may lie in cool comfort and watch the denizens of the forest, the chipmunks at play, perhaps if you look closely, there are elves beneath those mushroom stools. The tank battle seems far away because you are an elf and have things to do here . . . .

The schizophrenic may, for instance, be standing on the roadside thumbing a lift. Each time he is passed by, a surge of energy inflames his thoughts and feelings of insecurity, of rejection, of self-pity, so that these become entities on their own — vehicles for his consciousness. When he finally is offered a lift, he may not want it because one of these entities has presented a completely new set of interests, new scenery into which he quickly inserts his dramatic and current 'I'.

When the environment of the personality body becomes hostile, or in the absence of a strongly seated personality, he will try out other fragments of it or little 'I's', and like some histrionic person trying on new hats in front of the mirror, he will adopt and quickly dramatize himself into a new personality triggered off by the sight of himself in the hat.

All the disorders of speech (the incoherence, the over-discussion of irrelevancies, or the inability to comment at all) are part of this isolative procedure which leads him into more benign scenes wherein he may act out his life. The environment at home or in the office or anywhere need not be obviously hostile. The schizophrenic may be so sensitive to the presence of emotional currents, that he can sense them before most normal individuals can. He is ultra-sensitive, like Virginia Woolf, to the thoughts and feelings of others.

It is then that the genetically acquired factors in his brain and sensory mechanisms deal their cruellest karmic blow. The criticisms of others, though expressed only in thought or feeling, surface within the centre of his brain *as his own*, speaking through his own neurones, associated as they are with guilt or grandeur, symbol or phobia. This inner voice (which is very much a real phenomenon to the schizophrenic) will one day be recordable because it is ultimately a physical phenomenon! This is where it differs from that glorious inner voice (of the Silence) which is heard by the mystic and the man who, through meditation, establishes contact with his higher nature, his overself, or with the consciousness of higher beings.

The voice of the schizophrenic, especially in times of stress, advises him, cajoles him, comforts or berates. Because he is under tremendous stress, he is more receptive to the admonitions of this voice. He may feel that he should take a drive into the country to get away from the hostility about him. Immediately the voice intrudes: 'Yes, go on, go on, go on.' Or, according to the dramatized situation in which he is momentarily the central actor, it may interject with, 'Dirty coward, coward, coward.' And so on.

If the world outside is completely unbearable, he will begin to draw comfort from his voices; he will pay attention to them. If that world improves, or if he is blessed with a compassionate therapist or counsellor, then the voices will embarrass him and though they distract him, he may pay them no attention. Sometimes, in more spiritual individuals, the voice will blend in with a waking dream or vivid inner experience so that it may be given the status of a divine instruction or injunction, and this is the most heartbreaking manifestation of all delusion — the blending of the Real and the unreal:

From the unreal lead me to the Real.
From darkness lead me to Light.
From death lead me to Immortality.

In these circumstances, the schizophrenic may be aroused to take action, to crusade, to become an evangelist.

The mood may take him to regard his surroundings at times as benign, encouraging even a willing and applauding audience to whatever scene he wishes to act out. He may have just put down a book which has stirred him — some hero has caught his fancy — he *is* the hero. As he walks down the garden path, he acts out the Roman Triumph presented for his honour, his fierce brow bows to the waving multitudes on either side, the gardener waves to him and calls 'Hullo there!'. Immediately he turns frostily on him and from great heights answers grandly, 'Sir, how dare you address me in that fashion!' and is gratified by the laughter it provokes. As he continues down the path, he brushes aside a small hanging branch; the branch becomes a palm frond; the crowds start to call 'Hosanna. Hosanna in the highest.' He accepts their plaudits, now with the gentle mien of Our Lord — he will do something about the cramped conditions here in Jerusalem, after he has dealt with Pontius Pilate . . . Pilate with his innuendos — 'Publish and be damned', and immediately he is the Duke of Wellington, and that hedge is the serried ranks of his infantry squares; his taut face must not now betray to the men his misgiving about the arrival of that charlatan Marshall Blucher . . . and so on and so on.

This may occupy a matter of minutes or be spread over days or months. Not one of us has been exempt from having experienced some feature or the other of these delusions, especially in childhood and adolescence. All parents should read at least on of Richmal Crompton's 'William' books before they suspect their children of psychosis. In fact, in the supergifted child, imagination forms a great part of his play. The ability of a child to elaborate his own fantasies in connexion with any toy, to play endlessly with one toy for hours is usually indicative of a highly developed soul.*

The parents are powerful influences who can contribute greatly to the inhibition or, conversely, to the outward manifestation of schizophrenia in their offspring. The immature or non-synthesized personality of the schizophrenic child can suffer easily and severely from guilt or self-blame. If the child, as is often the case today, is brought up for the convenience of the parents (e.g., 'I thought having children would bring us closer together'), it may be made to feel guilty over things that inconvenience the parents: if the child soils himself, he is made to feel guilty; if he makes a noise when mother takes her rest each afternoon, he is admonished, etc.

Self-blame is crippling to such personalities, and these guilt

* See *Psychology of Discipleship*, pp. 73-116, by the present writer.

complexes may take years of psychotherapy in an institution to remove before the patient can be put on the path of sanity once more. It has frequently been observed by psychiatrists that when the father goes to hospital for some disorder, the schizophrenic son will show an immediate and marked improvement.

Any form of criticism, direct or implied, can be devastating to the equilibrium and stability of the patient. This is the reason why such vast sums of money are spent in providing ideal conditions in voluntary psychiatric clinics where a patient can seek refuge from his home, employment or family, thus avoiding the need for institutionalization.

This sensitivity to guilt can be stirred up by people whose attitudes to the schizophrenic show nothing but ignorance and callousness. Those who laugh and jeer should be made aware of the karma they are setting in motion, which could bring them back in a future life to the same set of circumstances which now incur their derision.

Without help, the schizophrenic can quickly deteriorate to the point of becoming irretrievable. None of us likes to live precariously, in poor occupations or as the target for derision. Yet, we have personalities that face up to such vicissitudes. The schizophrenic has not got this resilience of personality. Under pressure, he will over-react or, alternatively, sink into a world of his own and then display outwardly emotional and mental impoverishment and lack of coordination with his surroundings.

Karma of Schizophrenia

In previous lives the schizophrenic has been placed into circumstances which might have been favourable for the Soul's expression. On occasions, in an attempt to communicate its purpose to the personality, the Soul spoke to him inwardly. The individual was, however, unable to hear that inner voice — his attention being oriented almost entirely toward matters related to the outer, objective world. Ever-present were the demands placed upon him by business, pleasure, friends, family, and unwarily he pursued the beckonings of worldly desires for new experience, response, recognition and security. Distracted by the bustle and din of material living, he became a captive in the thraldom of objective experiences. Thus in so doing, he blunted his sensitivity to inner experiences, disallowing any notice of the urgings from his Soul.

Given a situation such as this, the Soul may, in an attempt to adjust this overbearing imbalance and insensitivity, choose a life which disposes the personality to schizophrenia. Now, in a life as a schizophrenic, there is an exaggerated emphasis placed on stimuli from *within*. Reality, in terms of outer expression, no longer exists! He may not even see, much less comprehend, the worlds which used to surround his personality and is faced with conditions where voices from within become paramount. Now the *inner* worlds command his attention, and he cannot resist their impression.

Treatment of Schizophrenia

At the outset, it cannot be stressed strongly enough that under no circumstances should shock treatment or insulin coma be resorted to. Both of these ghastly last-resorts have proved *utterly useless*. Both English and American psychiatrists concur on this point. You should campaign against their use under *all* circumstances.

Currently-employed psychotherapy is helpful and recommendable, especially when psychoanalysis is conducted by a humane and compassionate expert. Catharsis to bring out guilt and supportive therapy in the form of out patients' clinics, etc., go without saying. Under no circumstances should *acute* attacks of schizophrenia be dealt with by the esoteric healer. For the chronic schizophrenic, for prevention of onset, and for palliative treatment, the esoteric healer should use the following together:

(1)   Slippery Elm bark
(2)   The Satipatthana method

The latter, when practised in its simplest form, is nothing more than an exercise to bring out the 'I am' aspect of the patient's personality, to reduce the mobility with which the astral and mental bodies slip out of alignment with the hegemony of the central or basic personality.

The Satipatthana Method

If the esoteric healer would refer to my book *Meditation, The Theory And Practice* under the section 'Progressive Attrition', the Satipatthana Method will indicate the sort of therapy that the schizophrenic would be helped by — an exercise that should be modified and gently applied, with the central aim at linking the focussed mind to affairs of everyday living:

> The first important requirement in the task of learning to control the mind was to restrict its activity. Conscious control of the mind is under any conditions a difficult thing to achieve, but if during the attempts to do this the mind is allowed its full field of operation, it is impossible. It must in some way be restricted. We do this unconsciously when we are particularly interested in a thing to the exclusion of all else; and if effective restriction can successfully limit the mind's activities over a long period, it is possible for the will gradually to assume control. The whole secret of the success of the Satipatthana method lies in the selection of a natural field for these activities which, though restricted, offer the mind continuous occupation.
>
> The two basic exercises that I was given at my first interview were the beginning of this restriction process. I have mentioned earlier that the simple, sensuous pleasure that I derived from my morning tea walks had to be given up to the contemplation of the movement of my feet for every step of the way there and back. Very soon the actions of eating were included in the contemplative exercises. The mind had to follow the movement of the hands and arms in lifting the food to the mouth, and the actions of chewing, swallowing and drinking. Each consecutive action during the meal, from the first one of sitting down to the final wipe of the lips and getting up, had to be followed consciously without break. The greater the amount of detail that could be included, for example, tasting, and the feel of the cool water in the mouth, or the actual texture of the food that was being eaten, the easier it would be to keep the mind from wandering. It was not really as difficult as it sounds, once the initial disinclination to accept the task had been overcome. After this, the actions of getting up in the morning, washing, etc., and going to bed at night were added. It very soon became a habit to make my first conscious thought in the morning 'waking, waking' followed by a quick run round the senses to detect the touchings, sounds, etc., that they were receiving. Then came the action of sitting up, stretching out first one leg and then the other, getting out of bed, standing and so on. Each action of washing followed: stretching out the hand to turn on the shower, feeling the water on one's body, rubbing with the soap, drying, and then on the walk back to my cell 'lift, swing, down', until one arrived at the door, when actions of stretching, turning and pushing were necessary to enter the cell. It can be readily understood that the mind was indeed kept busy, and this close

attention to all the bodily actions continued.*

Slippery Elm Bark

Slippery Elm is synonymous with Rock Elm, Indian Elm, Sweet Elm, Moose Elm, American Elm and Red Elm. The following are physical symptoms which accompany the taking of Slippery Elm: Reduction in tension and increase in vital energy within a matter of hours. Ability to work longer and to focus the mind in sustained concentration. There is heightened muscle tone in the alimentary canal, although this action can be selective. The pyloric sphincter, for instance, may become excessively contracted and become a little unpleasant, but this soon passes. Bowel action is enhanced.

The action on the sympathetic nervous system gives sexual symptoms. The herb is contra-indicated in pregnancy through its action on the muscles of the uterus. In men there are no contra-indications for this anatomical area, but with enlarged prostate there can be a feeling of tension. It is interesting that the remnant of the uterus in the male is located as the utricle within the substance of the prostate gland. There is excessive tendency to erections in the early morning, reminiscent of youthful days.

Psychological symptoms accompanying Slippery Elm: The emotional and mental experiences both in the waking and dreaming state tend to shift the polarity of consciousness *away* from the metaphysical, *away* from the mystical, *away* from the path of discipleship towards the material world, towards the satisfying of the basic drives. Now this may be disconcerting to the esoteric student, to those who safely and progressively explore the inner worlds where attachments and earthly experiences are anathema, but for the schizophrenic, who slips into mystical, abstract states far too easily, the effects of Slippery Elm are most palliative and efficacious in pulling the patient out of psychotic states.

The dream life becomes frequented by paranoic experiences, and these tend to ease the outward urge to express them. There is more capacity to focus the mind and to relate thoughts to central ideas. The stimulation of the sympathetic nervous system potentizes the original and central personality,

---

* *An Experiment in Mindfulness* by Rear Admiral E.H. Shattock (Rider & Company, London).

giving it more identity and furnishing it with strong needs and urges.

The use of the herb is contra-indicated in hypertension. It will tend to raise the blood pressure, but usually only slightly, so that the hypertension must be severe for it to be dangerous to take Slippery Elm bark.

The student of esoteric psychology will understand what is intended here when I say that the 'I Am' is reaffirmed at the expense of the 'I Am That'. Needless to say, all forms of introspection — from meditation to day dreams — should be discouraged. The patient should be kept busy with gentle but interesting activities, hobbies and productive physical occupations especially.

How much? How often? When indicated? When terminated? These questions on the administering of Slippery Elm in relation to the treatment of schizophrenia have yet to be answered and only careful research by capable scientific bodies will tell. My own method, which I have tried with safety and with effective results, is to take a tablespoonful heaped with the bark and bring it to a boil in a pint of water. After allowing the mixture to simmer over a lowered heat for fifteen or twenty minutes, it is allowed to cool and then strained through a sieve. The resulting potion can be sweetened or flavoured with nutmeg or mixed with a suitable drink, soup or hot milk.

Most herbalists agree that it can be taken *ad libitum*, but as stated above, the most effective dosage for the condition of schizophrenia will depend on the research the healer has done. In the end, it is the patient himself and the psychotic signs and symptoms he manifests and progressively resolves that decide this issue.

Appendix I

Magnetism

In the field of low frequency waves, we have tried out in the Institute of Rheumatology at Rome University a generator of ultra-long waves with a frequency of 50 Hertz, known as the Magnetiser.*

The Magnetizer's principle is to generate a magnetic field round the emitting electrodes. These electrodes, being in opposition, start vibrating when the current is passed. Impulses are set up by a central block, into which further electrodes can be plugged with the possibility of treating multiple areas of the same patient simultaneously.

The physical characteristics have been checked by us at the Physics Institute of Rome University under the following conditions: supply tension 30 watts d.c., current consumption 300 milliamps. The following operations were carried out at different distances from the electrodes with these results:

At point A (1cm from the centre of the pole) 400 gauss.
At point B (3cm from the centre of the pole) 100 gauss.
In the field alongside the magnet (point C) at a distance of 1cm gave 20 gauss.

Further, given that the apparatus consisted of two magnets in opposition, beyond the magnetic field there was also set up by the attraction and repulsion of these same two magnets, a vibration at each reversal of polarity.

* Made by the firm of Kawasaki, Tokyo.

The equipment is composed of a fixed part and movable parts. The fixed part consists of an armchair in which are inserted at the height of the nape, back, pelvis and feet emitting blocks capable of functioning simultaneously or separately at two intensities: weak and strong. At the maximum intensity the physical performance is as already shown, and at the weak the values are about halved. The moving part consists of a series of insulated blocks, each comprising two magnets in opposition, with the same conditions of functioning and control and which can be applied to the respective areas of the limbs.

Our observations concern 40 patients with various rheumatoid conditions and at different stages, chosen in such a way as to make the therapeutic possibilities of the Magnetizer ascertainable. The treatments were applied once a day, using the armchair and one or more of the blocks in pairs, at maximum intensity. The use of the blocks in pairs was suggested to effect a better or more intense penetration of the tissues by the electromagnetic waves. The length of each application varied from a minimum of 15 to a maximum of 30 minutes, and the optimum number of treatments was established as between 20 and 30 sessions. In twenty-five patients it was noted at the start of treatment, as a side-effect, a sharpening of the pain which then disappeared as the treatment progressed. In the only two cases of rheumatoid arthritis the pain was satisfactorily reduced with a slight lessening of the swelling of the hands. Of the nine patients with cervical osteo-arthritis, two showed no improvement from the treatment, while the other seven experienced a slight lessening of pain. Of the two patients with periarthritis of the shoulder, one showed very good results and even the return of articulation, while the second showed no improvement. The two patients with lumbar pain showed a good result both in increased mobility and decreased pain. Of the ten patients with lumbar osteo-arthritis, one showed no improvement, while of the other nine, eight experienced a decrease in pain and one a good result. Of the three patients with pain due to disc pathology, two showed no improvement, while a third felt a good reduction in pain. Of three patients with arthritis of the knee joint, one of which had an effusion, the first showed no improvement, the second a good result with the ending of effusion, the third a poor result.

At the level of articular and periarticular tissues, in which acute inflammation was present, the beneficial effect of the therapy which we employed was particularly evident. The positive effects noted in several arthritic conditions are certainly the result of the analgesic and anti-inflammatory effect of the ultra-long electromagnetic waves and the vibromassage. During the experiments no disturbing side-effects, signs of intolerance, or reactions of a toxic or lesive order showed themselves. One may therefore affirm that the action of the ultra-long waves is to be considered harmless. Indeed, we may say that broadly speaking the patients who were treated with more blocks showed an improvement in general well-being. On the whole the patients felt more tranquil, became more mobile and increased their resistance to fatigue. This effect has already been demonstrated by Japanese writers in experiments carried out on fatigue in air pilots treated with ultra-long waves.

The mechanism whereby such therapeutic action might be explained is not yet clearly known. One can assume an action on the circulatory system causing an active hyperaemia and consequently a better blood-flow in the tissues, better nutrition from the increase in cellular metabolism, modifications of the tissue ph and general analgesic action on the nervous system. It is to be noted, furthermore, that the vibration produced by the apparatus could bring about a process of vasodilation, improving the peripheral blood-flow and consequently the cellular metabolism. The analysis of the therapeutic effects observed by us leads us to the conclusion that clinically the very long waves carry out their action principally by resolving local muscular contraction, thus attenuating the pain, though the intervention of other as yet unidentified mechanisms is not precluded. Such mechanisms would be explained by a better knowledge of the biological action of the long waves at a cellular level.*

---

* The above report, made by authors F. Dainotto and D. Tognazzi, was published in the *Recentia Medica*, Vol. V, No. 4, April 1966.